P9-DFV-618

SEEK THAT WHICH IS ABOVE

JOSEPH CARDINAL RATZINGER

SEEK THAT WHICH IS ABOVE

Meditations through the Year

Translated by
GRAHAM HARRISON

IGNATIUS PRESS   SAN FRANCISCO

Title of the German original:
Suchen, was droben ist:
Meditationen das Jahr hindurch
© 1985 Verlag Herder
Freiburg im Breisgau

With ecclesiastical approval
© 1986 Ignatius Press, San Francisco
All rights reserved
ISBN 0–89870–101–5
Library of Congress catalogue number 86–81553
Printed in West Germany

CONTENTS

CONTENTS

PREFACE

In this small book, at the kind invitation of
Herder Verlag, I am again setting before the
public a number of addresses which date
from my preaching activity in Munich. The
bulk of them were sermons and meditations
for Easter; to them I have added short radio
talks which were broadcast on various oc-
casions, both ecclesiastical and secular. As a
result, there is inevitably a certain amount of
repetition and overlapping, but this may help
to reinforce and deepen the same thought
from different sides and perspectives. Even
then, compared with the magnitude of the
issues raised, what I have said here is only
fragmentary. I hope, however, that the very
incompleteness and fragmentary nature of
these pieces may encourage the reader to
pursue his own thought and action along the
same path.

Joseph Cardinal Ratzinger

Feast of the Assumption of Mary
Rome, 1984

REFLECTIONS AT ADVENT

I

Memory Awakens Hope

In one of his Christmas stories Charles Dickens tells of a man who lost his emotional memory; that is, he lost the whole chain of feelings and thoughts he had acquired in the encounter with human suffering. This extinction of the memory of love is presented to him as liberation from the burden of the past, but it becomes clear immediately that the whole person has been changed: now, when he meets with suffering, no memories of kindness are stirred within him. Since his memory has dried up, the source of kindness within him has also disappeared. He has become cold and spreads coldness around him.

Goethe deals with the same idea as Dickens in his account of the first celebration of the feast of St. Roch in Bingen after the long interruption caused by the Napoleonic wars. He observes the people as they press, tightly packed, through the church past the image of the saint, and he watches their faces: the faces of the children and the adults are shining, mirroring the joy of the festal day. But with the young people, Goethe reports, it was otherwise. They went past unmoved, indifferent, bored. And he gives an illuminating explanation: they were born in evil times, had nothing good to remember and consequently had nothing to hope for. In other words, it is only the person who has memories who can hope. The person who has never experienced goodness and kindness simply does not know what such things are.

Recently a counselor who spends much of his time talking with people on the verge of despair was speaking in similar terms about his own work: if his client succeeds in recalling a memory of some good experience, he may once again be able to believe in goodness and thus relearn hope; then there is a way out of despair. Memory and hope are inseparable. To poison the past does not give hope: it destroys its emotional foundations.

Sometimes Charles Dickens' story strikes me as a vision of contemporary experience. This man who let himself be robbed of the heart's memory by the delusion of a false liberation—do we not find him with us today, in a generation whose past has been poisoned by a particular program of liberation that has stifled hope? When we read of the pessimism with which our young people look toward the future, we ask ourselves, Why? Is it that, in the midst of material affluence, they have no memory of human goodness that would allow them to hope? By outlawing the emotions, by satirizing joy, have we not trampled on the root of hope?

These reflections bring us straight to the significance of the Christian season of Advent. For Advent is concerned with that very connection between memory and hope which is so necessary to man. Advent's intention is to awaken the most profound and basic emotional memory within us, namely, the memory of the God who became a child. This is a healing memory; it brings hope. The purpose of the Church's year is continually to rehearse her great history of memories, to awaken the heart's memory so that it can discern the star of hope. All the feasts in the Church's calendar are events of remembrance and hence events of hope. These events, of such great significance for mankind, which are preserved and opened up by faith's calendar, are intended to become personal memories of our own life history through the celebration of holy seasons by means of liturgy and custom. Our personal memories are nourished by mankind's great memories; in turn, it is only by translating them into personal terms

that these great memories are kept alive.
Man's ability to believe always depends in
part on faith having become dear on the path
of life, on the humanity of God having manifested itself through the humanity of men.
No doubt each of us could tell his own story
here as to what the various memories of
Christmas, Easter or other festivals mean in
his life.

It is the beautiful task of Advent to awaken
in all of us memories of goodness and thus to
open doors of hope.

2

Dare to Step Forward toward God's Mysterious Presence

From early times the Church's liturgy has
set words from one of the psalms at the
beginning of Advent, words in which Israel's
Advent, the boundless waiting of that people,
has found concentrated expression: "To thee,
O Lord, I lift up my soul; O my God, in thee
I trust . . ." (Ps 24:1). Such words may seem
hackneyed to us, for we no longer attempt
the adventures which lead man to his own
inner self. While our maps of the earth have

become more and more complete, man's inner self has become increasingly a terra incognita, an alien region, in spite of the fact that there are greater discoveries to be made there than in the visible universe.

To thee, O Lord, I lift up my soul: recently I came to a new awareness of the dramatic meaning behind this verse when reading an account which the French writer Julien Green recently published concerning his path to conversion to the Catholic Church. He tells how, in his youth, he was in bondage to "the pleasures of the flesh". He had no religious conviction to restrain him. And yet, the strange thing is that, now and again, he goes into a church with the unadmitted longing for some miracle to happen that would instantly set him free. "There was no miracle", he goes on, "but, from afar off, the sense of a presence." This presence warms him and seems to offer hope, but he is still repelled by the idea of salvation being connected with belonging to the Church. He desires this new presence but is unwilling to undertake renunciation; he wants to effect his own salvation, as it were, and without any serious effort. Thus he encounters Indian spirituality and hopes to find in it a better way. But he suffers the inevitable disappointment and begins to examine the Bible. He is so in earnest about this that he starts taking Hebrew lessons from a rabbi. One day the latter says to him: "Next Thursday I won't be coming since it's a holy day." "Holy day?" asks Green in surprise. "The Ascension—do *I* have to tell *you* that?" answers the rabbi. The young man in his earnest search is suddenly struck as by a thunderbolt: it is as if the words of the prophets were raining down upon him. "I was Israel", he says, "whom God was entreating to come home." I felt the application to myself of the words, "The ox knows its owner, and the ass its master's crib; but Israel does not know . . ." (Is 1:3).[1]

This kind of experience of the truth of Scipture in our lives is what Advent is. This is what is meant by that verse, "I lift up my soul"; from being a hackneyed phrase it can become something new, adventurous and great if we begin to explore its truth.

Julien Green's account of his turbulent youth provides an amazingly accurate description of the struggles which our own age has to face. First of all there is the universal acceptance of the modern lifestyle, which on the one hand seems to us to be the inalienable form of our freedom yet is felt to be a slavery which it would take a miracle to abolish.

[1] J. Green, *Ce qu'il faut d'amour à l'homme* (Paris, 1978), 117f.

(And there is no question of the Church's old-fashioned ways being of any use here; the Church is not even regarded as an alternative. Exotic religions, by contrast, present a novel attraction.) And yet it is of great significance that the longing for liberation is not extinguished, that occasionally it asserts its influence in moments of quiet in a church. And it is this readiness to expose oneself to a mysterious presence, to accept it slowly and gradually, to allow it to penetrate, that enables Advent to take place, the first glimmer of light in however dark a night.

Sooner or later it becomes alarmingly clear: Yes, *I* am Israel. I am the ox that does not know its owner. And when, appalled, we get down from the pedestal of our pride, we find, as the Psalmist says, that our soul lifts itself up; it rises, and God's hidden presence penetrates ever deeper into our tangled lives. Advent is not a miracle out of the blue such as is offered by the preachers of revolution and the heralds of new ways of salvation. God acts in an entirely human way with us, leading us step by step and waiting for us. The days of Advent are like a quiet knocking at the door of our smothered souls, inviting us to undertake the risk of stepping forward toward God's mysterious presence, which alone can make us free.

Stepping out of the Night

What is Advent? Many answers can be given. We can grumble and say that it is nothing but a pretext for hectic activity and commercialism, prettified with sentimental clichés in which people stopped believing ages ago. In many cases this may be true, but it is not the whole picture.

We can say the reverse, that Advent is a time when, in the midst of an unbelieving world, something of the luminous quality of this lost faith is still perceptible, like a visual echo. Just as stars are visible long after they have become extinct, since their erstwhile light is still on its way to us, so this mystery frequently offers some warmth and hope even to those who are no longer able to believe in it.

We can also say that Advent is a time when a kindness that is otherwise almost entirely forgotten is mobilized; namely, the willingness to think of others and give them a token of kindness. Finally we can say that Advent is a time when old customs live again, for instance, in the singing of carols which takes place all over the country. In the melodies and the words of these carols, something of the simplicity, imagination and glad strength of the faith of our forefathers makes itself heard in our age, bringing consolation and encouraging us perhaps to have another go at that faith which could make people so glad in such hard times.

This latter kind of experience of Advent brings us quite close to what the Christian tradition has in mind with this season. It has expressed its view of Advent in the Bible texts which it took as the season's signposts. I will mention just one of them, a few verses from Paul's letter to the Christians in Rome. There he says, ". . . it is full time now for you to wake from sleep . . . the night is far gone, the day is at hand. Let us then cast off the works of darkness and put on the armor of light, let us conduct ourselves becomingly as in the day, not in revelling and drunkenness, not in debauchery and licentiousness, not in quarrelling and jealousy. But put on the Lord Jesus Christ . . ." (Rom 13:11–14). So Advent means getting up, being awake, emerging out of sleep and darkness.

There are many people, of course, who urge us to get up and awake; "Germany, awake!" was the cry of those who, years ago, were bent on deluding the nation; and today too there are awakenings and uprisings that lead further into darkness instead of out of it. What does Paul mean? He puts very clearly what he means by "night" by speaking of "revelling and drunkenness, debauchery, licentiousness, quarrelling and jealousy". For Paul, nocturnal revelling with all that goes with it stands for the dark side of human nature, man's being "asleep". For him it becomes a symbol of the pagan world as such, submerged in material things, held fast in the darkness that prevails where there is no truth and which, despite all its decibels and hectic activity, is asleep, because it lives unaware of genuine reality, of the real human vocation.

Nocturnal orgies as the image of a world in ruin—are we not appalled to see how aptly Paul characterizes our present times, which are returning to paganism? For us, "rising from sleep" means arising from conformity with the world and with the times and having the courage to believe and to shake off the dream that causes us to bypass our true vocation and our best possibilities. Perhaps the Advent hymns we hear every year may be lights to us, indicating our path, making us look up and recognize that there are greater promises than those of money, power and pleasure. Being awake for God and for other people—that is the kind of "waking" that

Advent has in mind, the wakefulness which discovers the light and brightens the world.

4

The Light of a New Humanity

Anyone who goes through our streets in the early days of December will often meet him, Santa Claus, dressed more or less as a bishop and never without his long white beard (which has been attributed to him since at least the eighth century). What these Santa Claus figures say and do is also more or less episcopal in nature; often they are more in the role of the bogeyman than of one who makes present the love of the Holy One, that love of which the legend speaks in many variations. It is almost impossible to tell with historical precision who this man was; and yet, by listening attentively to the oldest sources, through the mists of time, we can still discern the radiance of a figure who opens up a door to Advent, who can mediate, that is, an encounter with the reality of Jesus Christ.

In his portrayal of the life of St. Nicholas, his most ancient biographer, a certain Archi-

mandrite Michael, says that Nicholas received
his dignity from Christ's own sublime nature
just as the morning star receives its brilliance
from the rising sun. Nicholas was a living
imitation of Christ: "In the radiance of his
virtues", says the biographer, "the sun's right-
eousness has dawned."[2] Tradition has always
equated Santa Claus with the Bishop Nicholas
who participated in the Council of Nicaea
and, together with that first great assembly
of bishops, helped to formulate the affirmation
of the true divinity of Jesus Christ. What was
at stake here was the core of Christianity,
whether Christianity was to become just
another sect or something really new, faith in
the Incarnation of God himself. Was Jesus of
Nazareth only a great religious man, or had
God himself actually become, in him, one of
us? So, ultimately, the question was this: Is
God so mighty that he can make himself
small; is he so mighty that he can love us and
really enter our lives? For if God is too far
away from us to love us effectively, then
human love too is only an empty promise.
If God cannot love, how can man be expec-
ted to do so? In professing faith in God's
Incarnation, therefore, it was ultimately a
case of affirming also man's capacity to live

[2] L. Heiser, *Nikolaus von Myra. Heiliger der ungeteilten
Christenheit* (Trier, 1978), 7.

and die in a human manner. The figure of St. Nicholas, Santa Claus, illustrates and symbolizes this connection.

Theodor Schnitzler put this very well: "In putting his signature, in faith, to the mysterium of the incarnate Son of God, a person is enabled to be a helper of his fellow men, to bring happiness to children, families and the oppressed. Faith in the Incarnation promotes the salvation of mankind and the implementation of human rights."[3]

The oldest sources concerning St. Nicholas also point in the same direction from a different angle: Nicholas is one of the first people to be venerated as a saint without having been a martyr. During the persecution of Christians, those who opposed the pagan state power and gave their lives for their faith had quite automatically become great examples of faith. When peace was concluded between Church and state, people needed new models. Nicholas impressed them as one ready to help others. His miracle was not that of great heroism in the face of torture, imprisonment and death. It was the miracle of constant kindness in everyday life.

Another of the legends expresses it very beautifully in this way: Whereas all the other

[3] Th. Schnitzler, *Die Heiligen im Jahr des Herrn* (Freiburg, 1979), 22.

miracles could be performed by magicians and demons, and thus were ambivalent, one miracle was absolutely transparent and could not involve any deception, namely, that of living out the faith in everyday life for an entire lifetime and maintaining charity. People in the fourth century experienced this miracle in the life of Nicholas, and all the miracle stories which accrued subsequently to the legend are only variations on this one, fundamental miracle, which Nicholas' contemporaries compared, with wonder and gratitude, to the morning star reflecting the radiance of the light of Christ. In this man they understood what faith in God's Incarnation means; in him the dogma of Nicaea had been translated into tangible terms.

The morning star which receives its light from the rising sun—this ancient description of St. Nicholas is also one of the oldest images of the meaning of Advent. If we are to be continually lighting candles of humanity, giving hope and joy to a dark world, we can only do so by lighting them from the light of God incarnate. This, at the deepest level, is the message of all Santa Claus figures: from the light of Christ we are to light the flame of a new humanity, caring for the persecuted, the poor, the little ones—this is the core of the legend of St. Nicholas.

A light to enlighten the Gentiles
and the glory of thy people Israel.

Luke 2:32

Gentile da Fabriano, *Mary with Child* (15th cent.).
Photo: Helmuth Nils Loose.

CANDLEMAS

The Encounter between Chaos and Light

In everyday modern life we are hardly aware
that on February 2nd we celebrate an ancient
feast, common to the Church of both East and
West, which used to have a great significance
in the rural calendar: Candlemas. Tributaries
from many historical sources have flowed
together into this feast, with the result that it
sparkles with many colors. Its immediate
reference is to the event when Mary and Joseph
brought Jesus to the Temple in Jerusalem forty
days after his birth to perform the prescribed
sacrifice of purification.

The liturgy focuses mainly on one detail of
Luke's portrayal: the meeting between the
Child Jesus and the aged Simeon. Thus in the
Greek-speaking world the feast was called
Hypapanti (the encounter). In this juxta-
position of the Child and the old man, the
Church sees the encounter between the pass-
ing heathen world and the new beginning in
Christ, between the fading age of the Old
Covenant and the new era of the Church of
all nations.

What this expresses is more than the eternal recurrence of death and becoming; it is more than the consoling thought that the passing of one generation is always succeeded by a new one with new ideas and hopes. If that were all, this Child would not represent a hope for Simeon but only for himself. But it is more: it is hope for everyone, because it is a hope transcending death.

This brings us to a second aspect of this day which the liturgy illuminates. It takes up the words of Simeon when he calls this Child "a light to enlighten the Gentiles". Accordingly this day was made into a feast of candles. The warm candlelight is meant to be a tangible reminder of that greater light which, for and beyond all time, radiates from the figure of Jesus. In Rome this candle-lit procession supplanted a rowdy, dissolute carnival, the so-called Amburbale, which had survived from paganism right into Christian times. The pagan procession had magical features: it was supposed to effect the purification of the city and the repelling of evil powers.[4] To remind people of this, the Christian procession was originally celebrated

---

[4] Cf. *Der kleine Pauly. Lexikon der Antike* 1:297; also G. Martimort (ed.), *Handbuch der Liturgiewissenschaft* 2 (Freiburg, 1965): 290f.; G. Martimort, *L'Église en prière* 4 (Paris, 1983): 103f.

in black vestments and then in purple—until the Council's liturgical reform. Thus the element of encounter, again, was evident in this procession: the pagan world's wild cry for purification, liberation, deliverance from dark powers, meets the "light to enlighten the Gentiles", the mild and humble light of Jesus Christ. The failing (and yet still active) aeon of a foul, chaotic, enslaved and enslaving world encounters the purifying power of the Christian message.

It reminds me of something the playwright Eugene Ionesco wrote. As the inventor of the Theatre of the Absurd, he articulated the cry of an absurd world and was increasingly aware that it was a cry for God. "History", he said recently, "is a process of corruption, it is chaotic, unless it is oriented to the supernatural." The candle-lit procession in black garments, the symbolic encounter between chaos and light which it represents, should remind us of this truth and give us courage to see the supernatural, not as a waste of time, distracting us from the business of ameliorating the world, but as the only way in which meaning can be brought to bear on the chaotic side of life.

"FASCHING"—MARDI GRAS

The Ground of Our Freedom

Fasching—Mardi gras—is certainly not a Church festival. Yet on the other hand, it is unthinkable apart from the Church's calendar. Thus if we reflect on its origin and significance, it can contribute to our understanding of faith.

Fasching has many roots, Jewish, pagan and Christian, and all three point to something common to men of all times and places. It shows a certain correspondence to the feast of Purim in the Jewish calendar, which recalls Israel's deliverance from the menace of persecution of the Jews in the Persian empire, a deliverance brought about, in the biblical account, by Queen Esther. The joyful abandon with which this feast is celebrated is intended to express the feeling of liberation, and on this day it is not only a memory but also a promise: the person who is in the hands of the God of Israel is already, in anticipation, freed from the snares of his enemies.

But behind this exuberant, worldly feast, which had and still has a place in the religious calendar, there is also an awareness of that temporal rhythm which was given classical expression in the Book of Ecclesiastes: "For everything there is a season, and a time for every matter under heaven: a time to be born and a time to die; a time to plant and a time to pluck up what is planted; . . . a time to weep and a time to laugh; a time to mourn and a time to dance" (Qo 3:1ff.). Not everything is appropriate at all times; the human being needs a rhythm, and the year gives him this rhythm, both through creation and through the history which faith sets forth in the yearly cycle.

This brings us to the Church's year, which enables man to go through the whole history of salvation in step with the rhythm of creation, simultaneously ordering and purifying the chaotic multiplicity of our nature. Nothing human is omitted from this cycle of creation and history, and only in this way can all human reality, its dark side and its light side, the world of sense and the world of spirit, be saved. Everything finds its place in the whole, which gives it meaning and delivers it from its isolation. So it is foolish to want to prolong *Fasching* when business and one's agenda seem to recommend it: such extra time, artificially created by ourselves, turns into boredom; man is left alone as his own creator and feels truly forsaken. Then time is no longer the varied gift of creation and history but the monster which devours itself, the empty pre-occupation with sameness, whirling us round in a circle of meaninglessness, ultimately devouring us as well.

Let us go back to think about the roots of *Fasching*. As well as the Jewish, there is the pagan prehistory, whose fierce and menacing features still stare at us in the masks worn in Alpine, Swabian and Alemannic parts of Germany. What lie behind this are the rites for driving out winter and banishing demonic powers: the changes involved in times and seasons seemed to threaten the world's con-tinuance; it was necessary to secure the earth and its fruitfulness against the void to which, in the sleep of winter, the world seemed to come perilously close.

At this point we can observe something of great significance: in the Christian world the demonic mask becomes a light-hearted masquerade, the life-and-death struggle with the demons becomes fun and merriment prior to the seriousness of Lent. This masquerade shows us something we can often see in the psalms and in the prophets: it becomes a mocking of the gods, who no longer need to be feared by those who know the true God. The masks of the gods have become an amusing show, expressing the high spirits of those who can laugh at what once brought terror. To that extent, *Fasching* actually does contain elements of Christian liberation, the freedom of the One God, perfecting that freedom commemorated in the Jewish feast of Purim.

In the end, however, we are faced with a question: Do we still enjoy this freedom? Or is it not a fact that, ultimately, we would like to free ourselves from God, from creation and from faith, in order to be totally free? And is not the consequence of this that we are once again handed over to the gods, to commercial forces, to greed, to public opinion? God is not the enemy of our freedom but its ground. That is something we ought to relearn in these days. Only love that is almighty can ground a joy that is free from anxiety.

JOURNEYING TOWARD THE EASTER MYSTERY

I

Seek the Things That Are Above (Col 3:1)

"This is the day the Lord has made, let us rejoice and be glad in it": thus we sing in the words of one of the psalms of Israel, a psalm that had been waiting, in a manner of speaking, for the Risen Lord and so became the Easter hymn of Christians. We sing the Alleluia, a Hebrew word that has become a timeless expression of the joy of the redeemed.

But are we right to be glad? Or is joy not almost a kind of cynicism, a kind of mockery, in a world that is so full of suffering? Are we redeemed? Is the world redeemed?

The shots which murdered the Archbishop of San Salvador during the Consecration of the Mass are nothing more than a harsh search-light showing up the violence, the human barbarization, that has been unleashed all over the earth. In Kampuchea an entire people is being slowly wiped out—and no one wants to know. And everywhere we find that people are suffering for their faith, their convictions; their rights are being trampled on. Recently the Russian priest Dmitri Dudko, no doubt sensing that he would shortly be arrested, issued a message to all Christians, in which he says he is speaking from Golgotha, which is also the place where the Risen Lord appeared to the disciples behind locked doors. He sees Moscow as Golgotha, where the Lord was crucified, but also as the place where the Risen Lord becomes present and shows himself, in spite of (or even because of) the locked doors intended to keep him out.

Looking at the world, we may well wonder whether we actually have time to think of God and divine things, or whether we should not rather apply all our energies to improving the lot of people on earth. This was the attitude of Bertolt Brecht when he wrote:

> Do not delude yourselves with lies,
> Like the beasts man simply dies,
> and after that comes nothing.

He regarded belief in a world beyond, in the Resurrection, as a deception which hinders man from fully laying hold of this world, of life. But if we stress man's similarity to the animals and oppose this to his likeness to God, we shall very soon regard man simply as an animal. And if, as another modern poet has said, we die like dogs, we shall very soon live like dogs too, treating one another like dogs or rather as no dog should ever be treated.

The Jewish philosopher Theodor Adorno had a more profound view of things. In the passionate, messianic yearning of his people, he continually asked how a just world, how justice in the world, could be created. Ultimately he arrived at this insight: if there is to be real justice in the world, it must be for all and for all time, and that means justice for the dead as well. It would have to be a justice that retroactively heals all past suffering. And this would imply the resurrection of the dead.

Against this background I think we can hear the message of Easter in a new way. Christ is risen! There *is* justice for the world! There is complete justice for all, which is able retroactively to make good all past sufferings, and this is because God exists, and he has the power to do it. As St. Bernard of Clairvaux once put it, although God cannot suffer, he can be compassionate. And he can be compassionate because he can love. It is this power of compassion, springing from the power of love, which is able to make good the past and create justice. Christ is risen: this means that there is a power that is able to create justice and that is actively creating it. That is why the message of the Resurrection is not only a hymn to God but a hymn to the power of his love and hence a hymn to man, to the earth and to matter. The whole is saved. God·does not allow any part of his creation to sink silently into a past that has gone for ever. He has created everything so that it should exist, as the Book of Wisdom says. He has created everything so that all should be one and should belong to him, so that "God shall be all in all".

The question arises however: How can we respond and live up to these Resurrection tidings? How can this message come into our midst and become reality? For Easter is as it were the brilliance of the open door that leads out of the injustice of the world as well as the challenge to follow this radiant light and to show it to others, knowing that it is not a deluding dream but the real light, the genuine way out. But how can we get there? The answer is given in the Easter Sunday reading in which Paul writes to the Colossians: Christ is risen. Seek the things that are above, where Christ is. Set your minds on things that are above, not on things that are on earth (Col 3:1f.).

Listening with today's ears to St. Paul's exhortation to embrace the Easter message, the Easter reality, we are probably tempted to say, "So it *is* an escape into heaven after all; it *is* a flight from the world." But this is a crude misunderstanding. For it is a basic law of human life that only the one who loses himself finds himself. It is the person who tries to hold on to himself, unwilling to go beyond himself, who fails to find his own self. The man who wants to possess himself and does not give himself will not receive himself as gift. This fundamental law of human nature, which springs from the fundamental law of the love of the Trinity, from the very nature of the being of God (who, in giving himself in the form of love, is the true reality and the true power), applies to the whole realm of our relationship to reality.

It is precisely the person who desires only matter who dishonors it, robbing it of its greatness and dignity. The Christian honors matter more than the materialist does by opening it up in such a way that, here too, God may be all in all. The person who seeks only the body diminishes it. Desiring only the things of this world, he actually destroys the earth. We minister to the earth by transcending it. We heal it by not leaving it alone, by not remaining isolated ourselves. Just as the earth physically needs the sun in order to remain a life-bearing planet, and just as it needs the coherence of the universe in order to travel its path, so too the spiritual cosmos of man's earth needs the light from above, the integrating power enabling it to open itself up. We must not close the earth in upon itself if we are to save it; we must not cling to it greedily. We must throw its doors open so that the true energies by which it lives and which are so necessary to us can be present in it. Seek the things that are above! This is the earth's task: to live with a view to the world above, to live toward the heights, toward what is lofty and great, to resist the gravitational pull from below, the forces of disintegration. It means following the Risen One, ministering to justice, to the salvation of this world.

The first message of the Risen Lord, communicated to those who were his by means of the angels and the women, is: Come, follow me; I am going before you! Resurrection-faith is a stepping forward along the way. It can be nothing else than a following in the steps of Christ, a discipleship of Christ. In his Easter gospel, John has expressed very clearly where and how Christ has gone and whither we are to follow him: "I am ascending to my Father and your Father, to my God and your God" (Jn 20:17). He tells Magdalen that she cannot touch him now but only when he has ascended. We cannot touch him in such a way as to bring him back into this world, but we can touch him by following him, by ascending with him. That is why Christian tradition deliberately speaks not simply of following Jesus but of following Christ. We follow, not a dead man, but the living Christ. We are not trying to imitate a life that is past and gone nor to turn it into a program for action with all kinds of compromises and revaluations. We must not rob discipleship of what is essential to it, namely, Cross and Resurrection and Christ's divine Sonship, his being "with the Father". These things are fundamental. Discipleship means that now we can go where (again according to John) Peter and the Jews initially could *not* go. But now that he has gone before us, we can go there too. Discipleship means accepting the entire path, going forward into those things that are above, the hidden things that are the real ones: truth, love, our being children of God. Discipleship of this kind only happens, however, in the modality of the Cross, in the true losing of self which alone can open the treasury of God and of the earth, which alone releases, as it were, the living wellsprings of the depths and causes the power of real life to stream into this world. Discipleship is a stepping-forward into what is hidden in order to find, through this genuine loss of self, what it is to be a human being. It also means discovering that store of joy of which the world stands in such urgent need. Not only do we have a right, we also have a duty to rejoice, because the Lord has given us joy and the world is waiting for it.

Here is an illustration from recent times. The British doctor Sheila Cassidy (who in 1978 entered the Benedictine Order) was imprisoned and tortured in Chile in 1975 for having given medical treatment to a revolutionary. Shortly after being tortured she was transferred to another cell, where she found a tattered Bible. She opened it, and the first thing she saw was a picture of a man prostrate under lightning, thunder and hail. Immediately she identified herself with this man, saw herself in him. Then she looked further and saw in the upper part of the picture a mighty hand, the hand of God, and the text from the eighth chapter of the Letter to the Romans, a text that comes straight from the center of Resurrection-faith: "Nothing can separate us from the love of Christ" (8:39). And whereas at first it was the bottom half of the picture which she experienced, her being invaded by all that was terrible, crushing her like a helpless worm, she gradually came to experience more and more the other part of the picture, the powerful hand and the "Nothing can separate us".

At first she still prayed, "Lord, let me out of here", but this interior shaking of the prison bars turned more and more into that truly free composure which prays, with Jesus Christ: "Not my will, but thine, be done." Furthermore she discovered that, as a result, she was filled with a great freedom and kindness toward those who hated her; now she could love them, for she saw their hatred as *their* distress and imprisonment. Subsequently she was put together with Marxist women; she held services for them, and they too discovered this liberation from hatred and the great freedom which sprang from it. She says: "We knew that this freedom we had behind strong walls was not imagination; it was a quite tangible reality." After eight weeks she was released. What stayed with her, however, was that now she continually found Christ in everyday life, in people and in things. Thus she came to understand Chesterton when he described men and women who, signed with Christ's Cross, cheerfully walk through darkness. Finding this hidden life means releasing the sources of this world's energy, linking the world to the power that can save it, giving it the resources for which it seeks in vain within itself. It means digging for and uncovering the wellspring of joy which can save and transform things and people and which has the power to undo and make good past suffering. Seek the things that are above! This is not a mere clutching at a straw but a setting-out on the great Easter journey into the region of genuine reality.[5]

Recently I was deeply disturbed to read, in the words of an Indian woman missionary, that we are simply not in any position to show Christ to Indians, because most missionaries, totally taken up with exterior activity, are by Indian standards not really able to pray. This inability means that they in no way touch the point of the inner oneness of God and man; thus it is impossible for them to show the world the mystery of the Incarnate One and to lead the world to the freedom which comes from that mystery. This, then, is the first challenge of Easter: we are summoned to begin the journey inward and upward, toward the hidden, true reality, and we must find that it *is* reality. We can only have faith in the Risen One if we have encountered him. We can only encounter him by following him. Only if both things are true of us can we bear witness to him and carry his light into this world.

One of the psalms of Israel which the Church understands as a psalm of the Passion

[5] Cf. S. Cassidy, "Beten in Bedrängnis. Gebetserfahrungen in der Haft in Chile", in *Geist und Leben* 53 (1980): 81–91.

of Jesus Christ and which she long prayed at the beginning of every Mass is this: "Give me justice, O God." It is the cry of a world in the midst of suffering. Give me justice, O God! And he has said Yes. Christ is risen! What was past and beyond recall has been recalled. The power of transformation is available to us. Let our lives be one whole movement toward it! Let us seek the things that are above!

2

Not "The Cause of Jesus"—for Jesus Himself Is Alive

"On the third day he rose again", so we profess our faith with the Church in words that go right back to the primitive Jerusalem community, indeed right back to the preaching of Jesus, and that have their roots deep in the Old Testament. It is worth asking what is the significance of including this detail of timing in our profession of faith. First of all, Christendom wanted to establish the first day of the week with absolute certainty as the new day on which the victory of life took place; it wanted to stamp Sunday upon the mind of the world as the day on which a new reckoning of time began and to which all future time will relate. The Day of Resurrection is put into the Creed. It belongs to the center of Church faith and life. It is not an arbitrary arrangement but the day on which new life entered into this world.

Over and above this, the time reference "the third day" carries echoes of Old Testament ideas which help us to understand what resurrection means in our lives and in the times in which we live. In the descriptions of the Sinai Covenant, the third day is always the day of the theophany, i.e., the day when God appears and speaks. So the reference to the "third day" indicates that the Resurrection of Jesus is the conclusive event of the Covenant. It is the final, veritable entrance of God into history, making himself known to us in the midst of our world time, engraving himself upon it. Resurrection means that God holds the reins of history and has not handed over power to the laws of nature. It means that he has not become powerless and that the universal law of death is not, after all, the ultimate power in the world; he is the ultimate, for he is the first.

No doubt there is also in the background the idea that, in the East, corruption was thought to begin after three days, constituting the finality of death beyond recall. Thus Lazarus is expressly described as having already lain in the grave for four days; i.e., he had already begun to decompose. In this connection people would also have been aware of the Greek version of Psalm 16: "Thou lettest not thy beloved know decay." Since Christians knew in faith that these words of hope, remaining as yet unfulfilled in Israel's heart, had been fulfilled in Jesus, they knew that this hope-filled verse applied to him (Acts 2:25–33). The Resurrection on the third day was the answer to this hope, the affirmation that Jesus had not remained in the grave and in the jaws of death, but that in him the finality of death had been overcome by the finality of life.

So this time reference "on the third day", which initially seemed incidental, has given us a fresh understanding of what Resurrection has to say to us as a message for our time. First of all it means that the person of Jesus is more important than his "cause". In the sixties, people came up with the formula "the cause of Jesus goes on" as an interpretation of the Resurrection of Jesus. This, they said, was what the disciples had come to grasp "on the third day". But if this were all, merely the continuance of Jesus' "cause", we would have no more to say of Jesus than of

Marx and Lenin, Adenauer and de Gaulle. In
that case nothing really new would have taken
place in him; we would be left with the
melancholy resignation of Old Testament
wisdom: There is nothing new under the
sun. There is nothing behind apparent newness but the eternal succession of death and
generation and death. It would also mean
that everything people have thought and experienced and loved is doomed to disappear
into the inert silence of death, that ultimately
the earth's tiny civilization will be silently
extinguished among the infinite ocean of stars
and covered over by the sand of nothingness,
as Levi-Strauss put it.

"The cause of Jesus goes on." It says too
little. Indeed, it suggests something that is
quite false as well. For it would mean that it is
only causes, issues, that are abiding realities
in the world. Human beings come and go. It
suggests that they are only replaceable actors
on the stage of history, whereas history's
subject matter is what alone is permanent.
Thus people would be only servants of particular causes. The person would be a means,
and the cause would be the end. In such a
case, the person could be sacrificed for the
cause. Ultimately, all the cruel ideologies
which nourish scorn for the human being
(and we have been gathering their terrible

harvest throughout this century and since 1789) are based on this lack of respect for the person.

Recently I read this remark in a sermon: "Christ died for humanity's noblest cause." No. He did not die for a cause. He died for God and for mankind, and that is what constitutes God's victory and the victory for men. Causes do not continue to be noble once human beings are killed for them. The Risen One is the victory of the person, who is more than any cause, for God is person and has called man in his eternal love so that man may be eternal and so that his love may be eternal.

Furthermore the Resurrection of Jesus signifies the subordination of matter to spirit. We hardly dare say this today, for we are embarrassed by the way the human spirit has misused matter, creation. But such misuse comes precisely through things being given priority over the person. In this way the spirit becomes materialized, cold, thingly— and cruel. For it is in subordinating itself to matter that the spirit actually violates it, because the inner order of reality is interfered with. We have plenty of examples today of the spirit entering the service of matter and thereby deranging and destroying both. We need only think of the advertising business, where an enormous amount of intellectual acumen, intelligence and ideas is invested in order to seduce human beings into pre-occupation with mere matter. Or we can think of the investment in technology, which similarly expends vast amounts of spiritual energy, in its most highly wrought forms, in order to surround man totally with the world of matter. We find the same thing in the entire structure of our consumerist world: the goods we produce become masters of human beings. Man becomes the servant of the machine. Matter rules over him and subjects him to violence. Thus our century has become a century of great moral and material disaster for mankind.

It is all the more important, therefore, to profess the unabbreviated message of the Resurrection of Jesus. For if we exclude from it the body, matter, it means that tacitly we regard spirit and matter as eternally separate, that we hold matter to be unredeemable, that we exclude it from the realm and the power of God. Affirming the superiority of the spirit and of God over matter, as faith in the Resurrection implies, far from degrading matter and the body, actually guarantees its ultimate dignity, its redeemability, its being a part of God's single, whole creation.

Have you believed because you have seen me?
Blessed are those who have not seen and yet believe.

John 20:29

Jesus and the Unbelieving Thomas. Niello engraving on
the outside of a handled chalice (late 12th cent.) from
the monastery of Wilten. Vienna, Kunsthistorisches
Museum. Photo: Erich Lessing.

Resurrection-faith, therefore, is the most radical and dramatic denial of every form of materialism. But before we go on to speak of Marxist materialism, we ought to be quite clear that it is we who are providing opportunities for its undoubted ideals by the way we live in a materialist consumerism and pleasure-seeking that is devoid of all intellectual content, by the way we worship matter and thereby destroy and violate it. The Risen One ought to lift us anew out of such materialisms and bring us to the freedom of the spirit which also honors matter and allows it to be great.

Finally, the Resurrection of Jesus Christ is the affirmation of the priority of love and life over the strategies of the class struggle and the development of an envy-oriented consciousness, which is nothing but a strategy of death. Jesus Christ died, not "against" anyone, but "for" all. His blood does not call for more blood but for reconciliation and love, for an end to enmity and hatred. His Resurrection is the personified truth of the statement: love is stronger than death.

Consequently it does not matter, ultimately, who was historically guilty of the death of Jesus. Christendom has always known that this is not an issue, for the blood of Jesus Christ, as the Letter to the Hebrews says

(12:24), speaks more insistently than the blood of Abel; it speaks, namely, of forgiveness, reconciliation and love.

Hence the Holy Father, in his encyclical on the Redeemer of Man, has insisted that the Church has no other weapons but those of the Word and of love. So she cannot cease urging "Thou shalt not kill."[6] This is the challenge Easter sets before us. It also says: Do not become manipulators of power but servants of love in faith in the Risen One. For he is our certainty, in the midst of our experience of the powerlessness of the good, that love is the true and ultimate power in the world.

The Gospel at the Easter Vigil tells us that, after their encounter with the angels, the women started running, both in fear and in joy, to pass on the message to the others. Christianity is not something boring or second-rate; the person who is confronted with this message must start running. It sets him in motion because it is important that it should spread farther before it is too late. The apostles themselves began this race through the world, as it were, in order to bring to the whole of the known earth, in their generation, the message of the victory of life, of the

6 John Paul II, Encyclical *Redemptor hominis*, II, 16.

Lord's Resurrection. The disciples of Jesus slept that time on the Mount of Olives, but we slumber in the daylight of Easter Day and fail to see the central issue. In this hour we ought to open our hearts to the greatness of the message, so that we too may set off, bearing his light to others before it is too late, before death carries out its cruel harvest; fired by this day's joy, we ourselves ought to become evangelists, that is, heralds of the joy of Jesus Christ.

3

Judgment and Salvation

The Church's Paschal liturgy still enables us to experience something of that positively revolutionary joy with which people down the centuries have heard the gospel message in all its freshness: Christ is risen! In old chronicles we read how the faithful in Russia used to embrace each other with this greeting. They had undergone tangible renunciation during the period of Lent, and now that this period was over, they experienced a real, immense overflowing of joy. By entering into the rhythm of the Church's year they knew quite tangibly that life had triumphed and that life was beautiful.

We still celebrate Easter today, of course, but the grey veil of doubt has spread over the heart of Christendom, robbing us of joy. Doubt undermines the Paschal joy even in the very midst of the community of believers. Rudolf Bultmann has expressed the *angst* of modern Christendom in an extreme form. He was unable to imagine that anything had really happened, to the dead Jesus; but he went on to say this: Even if something had happened what would it signify? What good would "the miracle of a resuscitated body"— as he put it—do anyone? In less learned terms the question is, What is *one* resurrected body against the army of dead stretching back through the world's history? In the face of all the horrors of history, the light of Easter seems to dwindle to insignificance.

So is Easter obsolete, a word powerless to inspire hope? If we want to grasp the real meaning of Easter Day, we must, for once, put the question the other way round: what would it mean if Easter, the Resurrection of Jesus, had *not* taken place? Would it mean just one more corpse, insignificant among the statistics of world history, or would there be more to it? Well, if there were no Resurrection, the story of Jesus would have ended with

Good Friday. His body would have decayed, and he would have become a has-been. But that would mean that God does not take initiatives in history, that he is either unable or unwilling to touch this world of ours, our human living and dying. And that in turn would mean that love is futile, nugatory, an empty and vain promise. It would mean that there is no judgment and no justice. It would mean that the moment is all that counts and that right belongs to the cunning, the crafty and those without consciences.

There would be no judgment. Many people, and by no means only wicked people, would welcome that because they confuse judgment with petty calculation and give more room to fear than to a trusting love. This is the motivation for the passionate efforts made to remove Easter Sunday from the pages of history, to "get behind" it and stop history with Good Friday. But these escape attempts result, not in redemption, but in the dreary kind of joy of those who regard God's justice as something dangerous and therefore wish it did not exist. All this makes clear what Easter *does* mean: God has acted. History does not go on aimlessly. Justice, love, truth—these are realities, genuine reality. God loves us; he comes to meet us. The more we go along his path and live in his way, the less we need to fear justice and truth, the more our hearts will be full of Easter joy. Easter is not only a story to be told: it is a signpost on life's way. It is not an account of a miracle that happened a very long time ago: it is the breakthrough which has determined the meaning of all history. If we grasp this, we too, today, can utter the Easter greeting with undiminished joy: Christ is risen; yes, he is risen indeed!

4

"Be Lifted up, O Ancient Doors"
(Ps 24:7)

In a certain way the message of the Resurrection of Christ notably exceeds our faculty of imagination. It cannot enter into our minds at all as immediately as the message of Christmas. Birth is part of our experience, and it always involves elements of hope and joy. The story of God's Son, born in a stable as the Son of Man, has the power to speak to our hearts directly and can mean something even to the person who does not believe in the divinity of the Child. The Resurrection, however, lies beyond our experience; the only life we know is bound up with death. Rudolf Bultmann has most clearly put into words our inability to come to grips with the Easter message when he says: Even if this had happened, what would the miracle of a resuscitated corpse mean to us?

This is the question: Is the Resurrection of Jesus only an abstruse miracle that, even if it did take place, does not alter human nature? At this point the Church's liturgy tries to help us along by translating what we find inconceivable into images and forms that are familiar to us, or at least by providing an orientation for our hearts, pointing them toward Easter faith. The liturgy uses symbols like light and water; but above all it draws upon the great treasury of human suffering, prayer, doubting, wrestling and hoping contained in the Old Testament.

Out of the many biblical concepts which, since earliest times, the liturgy has used to illuminate the Paschal mystery, I will take just one which links both Christmas and Easter and thus manifests the inner unity of Christianity. We find it in Psalm 24 (23): "Lift up your heads, O gates! And be lifted up, O ancient doors! That the King of glory may come in" (v. 7). Our Advent hymn

"*Macht hoch die Tür*" ("Lift up your heads, ye mighty gates") comes from this psalm verse. Originally this whole psalm was part of a gate liturgy, an entrance liturgy. It was sung during the solemn entry of the Sacred Ark into the Temple. The intention was to invite God to dwell in this house, to live among men, to become their neighbor and fellow inhabitant. By entering a human house he would make it a house of God and use it to transform the world of men into the world of God. At the same time people were aware of how improbable, how impossible, such a project must seem, for no human house is big enough to house God. He far exceeds the dimensions of our human spaces; how could he possibly "enter in"?

It seems that the human world has no doors opening toward God. It is locked in upon itself. It is a prison, a house of the dead. People of the Old Testament and of other early civilizations initially applied the idea of the prison only to the world of the dead: the man who dies will not return. They imagined the underworld as a vast dark prison in which death reigns, a ruthless tyrant. It is a place of no return. Gradually, however, the feeling grew that, if all our paths lead to the prison which has entrances but no exit, then we are all prisoners. In that case even this present world is a house of the dead, the antechamber leading to a dungeon of horrors. And it is a fact: if death has the last word, the world *is* a waiting room leading to the void. Poets of our century have set down this feeling in terrifying visions. The Jewish poet Franz Kafka has probably gone farthest into this abyss of *angst*; his portrayal of a world of totalitarian control is intended as an interpretation of human life as such. In "The Castle", life appears to be a futile waiting, a doomed attempt to penetrate the maze of bureaucracy and reach some competent authority and hence freedom. In "The Trial", life itself is presented as a trial ending in execution. The story ends with the parable of a man who waits all his life outside a door and cannot get in, in spite of the fact that it was made especially for him.

If Christ is not risen, there is nothing more to be said about man than this; all else is merely an endeavor to deaden the pain. The cries of despair we hear and the cruel attempts at liberation we see are the necessary consequences of a world that will not accept Christ, its hope.

"Be lifted up, O ancient doors!"—these words of the psalm are not only liturgical symbolism, the gate liturgy of a long-past age. They are the cry of man in a world that is far too narrow, even if he can travel in spaceships to the moon and beyond. Christmas is only the first half of the Christian answer to this cry. Christmas tells us that there is not only the tyrant, Death: there is God, who is Life, and this God can and will reach us; he has broken a way in to us. He has found the door that was big enough for him, or rather, he has made such a door for himself. But this answer is only complete if there is not only an entrance by which God can reach us but also an exit for us. It is only satisfying if death is no longer a prison from which no one returns. And this is the content of the message of Easter. Not only is there a door in, there is also a door out. Death is no longer a house with no exits, a place of no return.

The ancient Church saw in this verse an interpretation of the article of faith "descended into hell", referring particularly to Holy Saturday, not as a word of mourning, but as a word of victory. The Church expressed this word in poetic form: the bolts of death's dungeon, of the world's dungeon, are wrenched off; the ramparts are thrown down; the gates are torn from their hinges. The one who has done this, Jesus, takes the long-imprisoned Adam and Eve, i.e., humanity, by the hand and leads them to freedom. Life is not a waiting room leading to the void but the beginning of eternity. The world is not the universal concentration camp but the garden of hope. Life is not the futile search for meaning, mirrored in the tangle of bureaucracy. God is not a bureaucrat; he does not live in a distant castle, nor does he hide himself behind impenetrable anterooms. The door is open; it is called Jesus Christ.

The celebration of Easter is intended to show us the radiant light which streams from this door. It challenges us steadfastly to follow this radiance, which is no will-o'-the-wisp but the brilliance of saving truth.

5

The Word of the Witnesses

The oldest account of the Lord's Resurrection to have come down to us is found in the fifteenth chapter of the first letter Paul wrote to the Corinthians. Scholars date this letter in the spring of the year 55 or 56. But the report of the Resurrection is older: Paul emphatically insists that the Corinthians, who wanted to cobble together their own version of Christianity, should stick to the words of the Creed handed down to them, and he quotes verbatim from the text to which he bound himself when he entered the Christian community. Precisely when and where this text originated is a matter of dispute. Some think it is possible to reconstruct an Aramaic original lying behind it and attribute it to the Aramaic-speaking Jerusalem community of the 30s; others believe it was formulated in Antioch at the beginning of the 40s.

However this may be, it speaks to us in the language of the beginning, like the speeches in Acts, that is, the language of those who were still eyewitnesses of what had happened and could be called to testify to what they had experienced. And we sense something of the profound responsibility on the part of those who proclaimed the message of Jesus Christ to be faithful to their message. Even Paul, who so emphatically stressed his independence from the original apostles and his own encounter with the Lord as the source of his gospel, does not construct a Christianity of his own but binds himself, down to the last word, to the common profession of faith. And he does this because two decisive features of faith require it: only in this way is the spatio-temporal unity of the Church guaranteed; and only in this way is the truth of what is testified assured, resting on faithfulness in the process of handing it on. By examining even the linguistic structure of 1 Corinthians, i.e., the tangible distinction between the word of tradition and Paul's own language, it is possible to ratify what 2 Peter says about the origin of Christianity: we did not follow cleverly devised myths but trusted the eyewitnesses who have seen God's great power (cf. 2 Pet 1:16).

Faith in the Risen One is faith in something that has really taken place. Today it is still true that Christianity is neither legend nor fiction, not mere exhortation nor mere consolation. Faith stands on the firm basis of reality that has actually taken place; today too, in the words of Scripture, we can as it were touch the Lord's glorified wounds and say, with Thomas, in gratitude and joy: My Lord and my God! (Jn 20:28).

One question, however, continually arises at this point. Not everyone saw the Risen Jesus. Why not? Why did he not go in triumph to the Pharisees and Pilate to show them that he was alive and to let them touch his scars? But in asking such questions we are forgetting that Jesus was not a resuscitated corpse like Lazarus and the boy of Naim. They were allowed to return once more to their erstwhile biological life, which sooner or later would have to end, after all, with death. What happened in Jesus' case was quite different: he did not return to the old life but began a new one, a life that is ultimate, no longer subject to nature's law of death but standing in God's freedom and hence final and absolute.

A life, therefore, that is no longer part of the realm of physics and biology, although it has integrated matter and nature into itself on a higher plane. And that is why it is no longer within the ambit of our senses of touch and sight. The Risen One cannot be seen like a piece of wood or stone. He can only be seen by the person to whom he reveals himself. And he only reveals himself to the one whom he can entrust with a mission. He does not reveal himself to curiosity but to love; love is the indispensable organ if we are to see and apprehend him.

This does not mean, however, that the person addressed by the Lord has to be a believer already. Paul was not, nor was Thomas, nor were the Eleven either, for they too were submerged in doubt and sorrow. The only victory they had in mind was the triumph of Jesus in the establishment of the messianic kingdom: the alternative was ruin. Resurrection such as they now encountered was not something they could imagine, nor was it what they were expecting. It was not a prior faith that created a Resurrection vision: rather it is the reality of the Risen One that creates faith where there was only disbelief or a cramped and grudging faith. What the Lord does require is a waiting readiness on the part of a heart that is open for service. Seeing must not remain just seeing; it must become love and witness.

There is another important aspect: Jesus shows himself in the act of departure. This is clearest in the event of Emmaus and in his meeting with Mary Magdalen. He summons us to go with him. Resurrection is not an indulgence of curiosity: it is mission. Its intention is to transform the world. It calls for an active joy, the joy of those who are themselves going along the path of the Risen One. That is true today too: he only shows himself to those who walk with him. The angel's first word to the women was, "He is not here; he is going before you to Galilee; there you will see him" (Mk 16:6). So, once and for all, we are told where the Risen One is to be found and how we are to meet him: he goes before you. He is present in preceding us. By following him we can see him.

6

In the Evening Tears, But Joy in the Morning

Since the most ancient times the Church has underlined her great feasts by not restricting them to a single day but giving them a whole octave of days. The celebration resounds for a whole week and is renewed on the eighth day. The seven days, completed by the eighth, symbolize the totality of time and its transcendence into eternity. The week-long feast encompasses a basic unit of human life and thus stands as a foretaste of the freedom of eternal life, a sign of hope and peace in the midst of earthly days of toil. The Church has endeavored to help us experience Easter as the feast of feasts, as the basic reason for all celebration and all joy, by causing the Easter octave to last for seven times seven days. So the feast of Pentecost on the fiftieth day after Easter is not in fact an entirely new feast; it rounds off the circle of the seven times seven days which signify our breaking out of subservience to time into the boundless joy of the children of God, a joy uninterrupted by any striking of the hour.

These fifty days of joy are the answer to the forty days of tribulation and preparation by which the Church leads up to Easter. In Old Testament numerology, forty signified the age of the world: it is an intensification of four, which recalls the four corners of the earth and hence the brokenness, the finite, incomplete and toilsome nature of all earthly existence. The forty prepare for the fifty, the fragmentary for the complete; and the

Lord's Resurrection is at the axis of both. Even through this temporal arrangement the Church has provided a profound psychological interpretation of what Easter means and of how we can and should celebrate it. For all these things, far from being liturgical games, are translations of the mystery in terms of our life; they are where the unique and once-and-for-all Event meets life in its daily newness.

I would like to elaborate on this by referring to another psalm which plays a part in the liturgy of Holy Week. In Psalm 30 the believer speaks with gratitude of his experience of God: "His anger is but for a moment, and his favor is for a lifetime. Weeping may tarry for the night, but joy comes with the morning." For Christians these words, read on Holy Saturday, gained an entirely new significance. In the evening tears, but joy in the morning: they saw the evening of Good Friday, the weeping Mother with her dead Son in her lap. But as an answer to this evening picture, in the dusk of history, there comes the morning picture: "The Lord is risen and is going before you into Galilee."

The other words are interpreted similarly: his anger is but for a moment, and his favor is for a lifetime. The somber moment of the Cross gives way to everlasting life; the moment yields to eternity. The forty days are followed by the fifty, the fragmented by the whole, the momentary by the everlasting and indestructible, the tears of the evening scene by the morning of full life.

Those who read Holy Scripture in a reflective spirit found this experience in Paul, translated into the profession of Christian hope: "I consider that the sufferings of this present time are not worth comparing with the glory that is to be revealed to us" (Rom 8:18). The center of gravity of existence has shifted as a result of this certainty: now it lies at the morning of life, which means that it takes away the oppressiveness and the pressure of the moment and dissolves the tears of evening by the power of a grace which lasts for ever. This is precisely what Easter faith is designed to give us: the ability to look across from the evening to the morning, from the part to the whole, and thus to journey toward the joy of the redeemed which springs from that morning of the third day which first heard the message: Christ is risen!

THE FEAST OF THE SPIRIT

I

Be Awake to Receive the Power
That Comes out of Silence

Pentecost and the Holy Spirit—ever since Christianity first existed, these concepts have exerted an almost magnetic attraction, and especially in our own day this attraction spreads far beyond those whose faith attaches them to the Church. First of all, naturally enough, it was the experience of the earthly Church, with all her limitations and her all-too-human sides, that continually nourished the yearning for a Church of the Spirit, of freedom and love. This begins with the Montanist preachers of the second century and can be detected throughout history, right up to the hopes and desires that accompanied the Second Vatican Council.

In the High Middle Ages, in Calabria, Abbot Joachim of Fiore developed a form of this expectation which grew like a veritable avalanche from century to century. He taught that the first kingdom of the Father would be succeeded by the second, that of the Son, and this in turn would be followed by the third kingdom, that of the Spirit, in which no external law or ordinances would be necessary any longer because the Spirit and love would lead man to freedom and render all external rule obsolete. Since the twelfth century this vision has continued to inspire theologians, philosophers and politicians. The first medieval attempts to reestablish the Roman Republic against papal rule in Italy cited the prophetic Abbot in their support. Even in our own time Il Duce, of unhappy memory, became acquainted, in a Geneva lecture hall, with the teachings of the medieval Abbot and wanted to be the one to carry them out. But Hegel too was aware of the inspiration that had come to him from Joachim; thus we can follow the thread (albeit a thin one) reaching from Joachim to the Marxist hope of a classless society from which alienation and exploitation will have been banished.

So there are countless variations on the theme of the Holy Spirit, at one extreme going so far as to hope that we will be able to erect the Kingdom of the Spirit as a kingdom of matter. But what *is* the message of Pentecost? How did the Church which proposed the topic of Pentecost respond to the varia-

*And there appeared to them tongues as of fire,
distributed and resting on each one of them.
And they were all filled with the Holy Spirit.*

Acts 2:3–4

The Descent of the Holy Spirit. Book of Gospels from
Great St. Martin's, Cologne (c. 1230), Ms 466/9222,
fol. 107r. Brussels, Bibliothèque royale Albert Iᵉʳ.

tions of it which, for the most part, were in effect antagonistic to her? Has the Church anything relevant to say today on this issue, anything that might be of significance beyond the circle of her closer adherents? It is hard to provide a convincing answer at the level of the original, received faith, becàuse the latter does not exhibit the same visibility as do concrete hopes and programs for action.

In the Gospel of John we can see how early people began to feel this dilemma; questions of almost alarming realism raise their heads in the midst of passages of often unfathomable profundity. Thus, for instance, while Jesus is delivering his farewell words, Judas Thaddeus suddenly asks, "Lord, how is it that you will manifest yourself to us and not the world?" (14:22).

This is the question that we too still ask ourselves: Why did the Risen Lord only appear to the circle of his disciples instead of appearing in power before his enemies and thus crushing every doubt? Why, through history, does he only let people feel their way toward him laboriously, through the word of the Gospel, instead of unambiguously setting up a kingdom of the Spirit and of love? Jesus' answer in the Gospel of John is very elusive. Augustine formulated it like this: It is because only the one who has the

Spirit can see the Spirit. He recalls a phrase of
the philosopher Plotinus whom he greatly
revered and which Goethe translated thus: If
the eye were not sun-like, it could not recognize the sun.

But let us ask again, what are Pentecost
and the Holy Spirit all about? We cannot
reveal the Spirit directly, so all we can do is
try, by means of images, to lead toward what
is meant.

Since ancient times the Church's liturgy
has found a helpful picture in Psalm 68 (67).
As early as the Letter to the Ephesians (4:7)
this psalm was understood as a song of
triumph for Christ's Ascension and hence as
a portrayal of the connection between Easter
and Pentecost. Verse 18 says, "Thou didst
ascend the high mount, leading captives in
thy train and receiving gifts among men".
According to the interpretation of the apos-
tolic letter, this means that Christ is the
Messiah, a victorious King, who has fought
and won the decisive battle of world history,
the battle with death. Now he exercises the
victor's right to distribute the spoils of war.
But what are these spoils? The answer comes:
The gift of God is God himself, the Holy
Spirit.

Men have always found this both too
much and too little. True, Israel had been

awaiting a victor who would fight battles
and bring back undreamed-of booty to the
Chosen People. But *this* battle—the Cross—
and *this* booty, the Holy Spirit as a power in
those who believe, this was a disappointment.
This was not what people had been waiting
for. They turned away, looked for and found
other messiahs who fought fierce and des-
perately heroic battles against the Roman
overlordship and who ultimately only caused
the land to be laid waste. Death took the
spoils of war; death was the real victor of
those decades of fighting.

And what about Christianity, what about
us, here and now? We too would expect quite
different gifts from a Redeemer from those
Paul describes. For we would expect a house,
money, good food, travel, success, other
people's esteem, comfort, peace, security.
But not the Holy Spirit. For in reality the
Holy Spirit is largely the opposite of all these
things: he makes us restless with our possessions, our comfort, our respect that is so
often based on dubious compromises. He is
a tempest. He does not let us settle down in
our comfort but exposes us to ridicule by
putting us in the service of truth and obliging
us to exercise the self-control which loves the
other person "as myself". He teaches us quite
a different redemption from that of the Third

Reich and of all earthly paradises. And yet, this tempest that frees man from himself and makes him true and kind, is it not the most radical of all revolutions, the only real hope for the world?

Now the question arises, however: Is this not a contradiction? On the one hand we are told that the Holy Spirit is something that cannot be exhibited; that he is invisible in a profound sense, like love, which affects man at a fundamental level and remolds him but which cannot be demonstrated like a new car. And on the other hand we hear that the Holy Spirit is tempest, transformation, so much so that he is described as the energy of the new creation, whose effect on reality is precisely that of "creating". How can this be? Well, we already have the answer in a nutshell in our reference to the love which cannot be proved and yet is the basic energy of human life and indeed of all reality.

A parable may help to make it clearer. A few years ago there was an impressive film entitled "The Transmigration of Souls". It was about two poor wretches who, because of their good-naturedness, could not improve their lot. One day one of them hits upon the idea of selling his soul, since he has nothing else left to sell. It is sold cheap and packed up in a box. From this moment, to his absolute amazement, everything in his life changes. He climbs fast, gets more and more wealthy, attains high honors and dies as a consul, well furnished with money and possessions. The moment he got rid of his soul, he lost all consideration, all humanity. Now he acts without scruple simply for profit and success. The human being is no longer of any account (and he himself has no soul). In a deeply moving way the film shows how, behind the facade of the successful man, there is an empty existence. On the surface nothing seems to be missing—but the soul has gone, and everything else along with it.

It is true, of course, that the human being cannot really throw away his soul, i.e., what makes him human. He is and remains a human being. And yet he has the terrible ability to be an inhuman human; while remaining human he can barter away his humanity and lose it. The gap between the human and the inhuman is vast and yet cannot be proved; it is the decisive factor, yet on the surface it seems of slight significance. To me, this is a parable illustrating much of what is involved in Pentecost.

Whether the Holy Spirit, the gift of the new creation, enters a man or not, whether a man makes room for him or not, is not something that can be seen or verified from the outside. It does not seem to have any relevance. And yet it is something that opens up a new dimension of human life that ultimately determines everything else. The point of Pentecost, therefore, is not to make us dream of better future worlds, let alone to encourage us to adopt a strategy of the future, thoughtlessly sacrificing the present for some supposedly future chimera. On the contrary, these days are meant to awaken us to the present hour, to the silent energy of divine goodness which is knocking at the door of our being and wanting to refashion it. To be awake to receive the power that comes out of silence—is this not a task and a hope which could be embraced by Christians and non-Christians alike, a Pentecost for all?

2

Think of Acting according to the Spirit

Most of the great festivals of the Church are rooted in the faith of Israel, and Israel's festivals, in turn, originate in the festivals of nature-religion in the world of peasants or nomads, from which the distinctive and new elements of Old Testament religion gradually developed. Thus these days of celebration are heavy with the burden of a long history, and that is what is so beautiful about them: they bring us forth out of the superficiality and bustle of our everyday life and leisure activities (which we begin to find more and more boring, because they always present us with the same old thing, namely, our own inventions; what we dream of, the discovery of an entirely different realm, never happens). The Christian festivals are more than "time off"; that is why they are indispensable: they present us, provided we have our eyes open, with the entirely other, the roots of our history, mankind's primal experiences and, through them, eternal love, which is man's real cause for celebration.

Let us take a closer look at this as we find it in the feast of Pentecost. From its earliest prehistory it has been a feast of harvest. In Palestine the crops were ripe in May; Pentecost was the thanksgiving for the grain harvest. Man sees the fruitfulness which results from the interplay of heaven and earth as the miracle by which he lives, and he acknowledges that gratitude is the appropriate response to this miracle. Thus harvest becomes a festival.

Has this become meaningless today? If we think of "Holy Spirit" only in terms of

Christian inwardness, and of "harvest" only in terms of technology and commerce, our view of the world has become schizophrenic. At Pentecost the Church prays a verse from the psalms which runs: Send forth your Spirit, O Lord, and renew the face of the earth. Initially this refers to the creative Spirit which has called the world into being and maintains it in being. It is important to have a new realization of this at Pentecost: the Holy Spirit who came down upon the apostles is the same Spirit who fashioned the world. The problems of our time are attributable in good measure to the fact that we have regarded the world as mere matter and matter as mere raw material for the production line. We need not be surprised that a world that is nothing but matter is becoming uninhabitable. Yet at the same time science is teaching us, in a way we could not have guessed, how spiritual matter is, a mathematics so subtle and magnificent that our own spirit can only look on in astonishment. Thus it is actually science that has rendered the wonderful logic of the Creator Spirit almost tangible to us.

Pentecost should also be for us a festival of thanksgiving for creation, a cause for reflection on the creative Reason which is also manifested in the beauty of the world as a creative Love. Thanksgiving for creation could then become a reflection on creation, a reflection on behavior appropriate to our being part of creation. This would be acting according to the Spirit, turning away from the practical materialism that abuses and destroys the world.

Against this background we must also understand that, in Israel, Pentecost was the remembrance of the arrival at Sinai and the celebration of the Covenant which had set out a path for Israel to travel in the form of the law. Christians have always seen their Pentecost as a continuation of this idea: the New Law is love, breaking down barriers and uniting people in the New Covenant. Love, too, is not formless or arbitrary; it is a formation from within, a wakefulness of the heart which takes up the rhythm of creation and perfects it.

The creative Spirit who called the world into being, the Spirit who became Word in the Sinai Covenant and the Spirit given to the apostles on the Day of Pentecost belong together: it is all one and the same Spirit. Pentecost, seen as the beginning of the Church, is an expansion of God's Covenant to all creation, to all nations and times. The whole of creation is brought into the sphere of the

Covenant; only thus can it achieve its real goal, which is to be a place where love is at home.

Some time ago it might have seemed highly anthropomorphic, not to say anthropocentric, when Paul says that creation waits with eager longing for the revelation of the sons of God (Rom 8:19). But today we can sense the groaning of creation under the feet of those who no longer have anything to do with God and want to delete him from the world. Creation cries out to the sons of God, for it was created with a view to the Covenant. The Holy Spirit of love is and remains the Creator Spirit "without whom nothing is in man, nothing is wholesome" (Pentecost Sequence). Thus Pentecost will be all the more a festival of creation, thanksgiving for it and a renewal of it, the more we experience it as a festival of Covenant renewal, the more we become the Church, nourishing ourselves from what is the Church's foundation and true nature: "A new commandment I give to you, that you love one another" (Jn 13:34).

WHAT CORPUS CHRISTI MEANS TO US

If we want to understand what Corpus Christi
means, we need only look quite simply at the
liturgical form in which the Church interprets
and celebrates this festival. Over and above the
elements it has in common with all Christian
feasts, there are primarily three structural
elements which constitute the distinctive
festal form of this day. First of all there is the
gathering together around the Lord, in which
we stand in commitment before the Lord and
in the presence of each other. This proceeds
then to a walking with the Lord, to the
procession, and finally to the kernel and goal
of the whole celebration, namely, kneeling
before the Lord, adoration, giving him glory
and rejoicing in his nearness. Let us examine
in more detail these three structural elements.

Standing before the Lord

In the Church of former times the word for this was *statio*. In referring to the *statio* we actually touch the most ancient root of what takes place at Corpus Christi and what it means. From the very beginning, when Christianity spread throughout the world, its heralds laid the greatest importance on there being only one bishop and only one altar in every town. This was meant to express the unity of the one Lord who unites us all in his embrace from the Cross, an embrace that goes beyond the frontiers drawn by earthly life and that forms us into one body. And this, of course, is the innermost meaning of the Eucharist, that, by receiving the *one* bread, we actually enter into this *one* center and thus become a living organism, the *one* body of the Lord.

The Eucharist is not a private matter among friends, taking place in a club of like-minded people where congenial spirits meet together. On the contrary, just as the Lord allowed himself to be crucified publicly outside the city walls, stretching out his hands to all, the Eucharist is the public worship celebrated by all whom the Lord calls, irrespective of who they are. So it is an essential contituent of the eucharistic celebration, just as it was a feature of the Lord's earthly life, that people of different party groups, different classes and views are brought together in the larger context of his word and his love. It was fundamental to the Eucharist in the Mediterranean world which first saw the growth of Christianity that the aristocrat who had found his way to Christianity should sit down with the Corinthian dock-worker, the miserable slave who, according to Roman law, was not even held to be a human being and was dealt with as chattel. It is of the very nature of the Eucharist that the philosopher should sit beside the illiterate man, the converted prostitute and the converted tax-collector beside the ascetic who has found his way to Jesus Christ. We can still discern, in the documents of the New Testament, how people continually tried to resist this kind of inclusive fellowship and wanted to enclose themselves in their own circle, and we can also see how the Eucharist asserted its meaning all the more, namely, to be a focus of assembly, transcending barriers and leading men into a new unity in the Lord.

When Christians increased in numbers, it was no longer possible to maintain this restriction to a single Eucharist and a single altar in the towns. In Rome, for instance, even during the era of persecution, the titular churches came into being as predecessors of the later parishes. This did nothing to minimize the public nature of worship, nor did it render it any more a matter of personal choice: the Eucharist continued to unite people who would otherwise not mix. However, the space-transcending aspect was no longer sufficiently visible. Consequently the *statio* was introduced: here, particularly during Lent, the Pope, as the single Bishop of Rome, goes among the individual titular churches and celebrates the liturgy for the whole city of Rome. Christians gather together and go to church together; thus, in the individual churches, the whole Church is visible and is manifest at the individual level.

Corpus Christi takes up this fundamental idea. It is *statio urbis*: we go beyond the parish church, we go beyond our usual custom and come from the different corners of the town in order to gather around the Lord, in order to be one in him. We come together beyond party and class boundaries, beyond the distinction between rulers and ruled, manual workers and intellectuals, people of this or that walk of life. And the essential thing is that we are gathered here by the Lord, that he has led us to each other. We should go forth from this hour, challenged to accept one another inwardly too, to open ourselves to one another, to go to meet each other; we should carry with us, into the manifold pre-occupations of daily life, this inner reality of having been gathered together by the Lord.

We all know that our cities have become places of unheard-of loneliness. People are never so alone and forgotten as in the huge tower blocks where they are crushed together. A friend told me that he had taken an apartment in one such block in a North German city. Going out of the block one day he greeted a fellow inhabitant; the man gave him an astonished look and said, "I'm afraid you're mistaken." Where people are lost in the mass, a greeting becomes a mistake. But the Lord gathers us together and opens us so that we can accept one another and belong to one another, so that, in standing side by side with him, we can learn once again to stand together with one another. It is precisely in this way that our Marienplatz in Munich fulfills its most profound function. How often we rush past each other here! Today it is a place where we are together in fellowship; let us carry this fellowship with us as both a gift and a task.

There are many kinds of gatherings of people, but so often they are united by what

they are *against* rather than by what they are
for. And almost always what brings them
together is some interest that seeks to defeat
other interests. Today, however, what binds
us together is not the private interest of this
or that group but the interest which God
takes in us. And we can calmly and confi-
dently entrust all our interests to him. We
commit ourselves to the Lord. And the more
we commit ourselves to the Lord and stand
before him, the more we stand together with
one another and the more power we discover
to understand each other, to recognize each
other as human beings, as brothers and sisters.
In this way, in this fellowship with one
another, we are building the foundations for
humanity and making it possible.

2

Walking with the Lord

From the outset, this standing together by
the Lord and with the Lord presupposed and
called forth a going toward the Lord. For *in
fact* we are not, of ourselves, with him. So
there could only be a *statio* provided that
people assembled together beforehand and

went together in procession. This is the second
call issued by Corpus Christi. We can only
come to the Lord by means of this procession,
this proceeding, by going out and going forward, by going beyond our own prejudices,
limits and closed areas, and walking toward
him, where we can meet one another. This
applies in the area of the Church as in the
world. For today, alas! we know division,
strife and suspicion in the Church as well.
The procession ought to be a challenge to
us to go forward toward him, together sub-
mitting ourselves to his standards and, in a
common faith in the Incarnate One who gives
himself to us in the form of bread, learning to
trust one another again, to open ourselves
to each other, and, in fellowship with one
another, letting him lead us.

The procession, which was already part of
the station Mass in Rome in early times, has
acquired a new dimension, a new depth, in
Corpus Christi. For now the Corpus Christi
procession is not simply a going toward the
Lord, toward the celebration of the Eucharist;
it is a going *with* the Lord. It is itself a part of
the eucharistic celebration, a dimension of
the eucharistic event. The Lord, who has
become our bread, actually shows us the
path; he *is* our path and leads us along it.

In this way the Church has given a new

interpretation of the story of Exodus, of Israel's desert wanderings. Israel journeys through the desert. It is able to find its way in the trackless wastes because the Lord, in the forms of cloud and light, leads it. It can live in trackless and lifeless places because man does not live by bread alone but by every word that comes from the mouth of God. Thus this history of Israel in the desert reveals the deepest reality of all human history. This Israel was able to find a homeland, and to survive the loss of this land, because it did not live by bread alone. It found in the Word the vital energy of a life that could go on through centuries of uncharted wanderings and homelessness. So Israel is for ever a sign raised up for all of us.

Man only finds his way if he lets himself be led by him who is both bread and way. Only by walking with the Lord can we survive the pilgrimage of our history. Thus Corpus Christi interprets our whole life, the whole history of this world: it is a pilgrimage to the Promised Land, and it can only hold its course if it is a walking with him who has come among us as bread and Word.

More than other ages, we know today that, in fact, the whole life of this world and the whole history of mankind is movement, ceaseless change and forward motion. The word *progress* has acquired an almost magical ring to it. But we also know that there can only be meaningful progress if there is a direction in which we are to go. Mere movement, by itself, is not progress. It can equally be a lurch into the abyss. So if there is to be progress, we must ask how it is to be measured and what is its goal. At any rate it cannot be a mere increase in material goods.

Corpus Christi interprets history. It provides our wandering through the world with a standard, Jesus Christ, the Incarnate One, the eucharistic Lord, who shows us the way. It does not mean, of course, that all our problems are solved. That is not what God's actions are designed to do. He gives us our freedom and our faculties so that we should exert ourselves, toiling to discover solutions. But the basic standard is given. And if we find in him the measure and the goal of our journeying, we have a way of distinguishing the direct route from the circuitous path. This day bids us walk with the Lord.

Kneeling before the Lord

Finally we come to kneeling before the Lord: adoration. Since he himself is present in the Eucharist, adoration has always been an essential element of it. Though adoration did not develop into this great festal form until the Middle Ages, neither change nor deviation is implied: it is nothing but the full emergence of something latent. For if the Lord gives himself to us, our receiving of him cannot but be a bending before him, a glorifying and adoring of him.

Nor is it contrary to the dignity, freedom and greatness of contemporary man to bend the knee, to pledge obedience to him, to adore and glorify him. For if we deny him lest we should have to worship, all we are left with is the eternal necessity of matter. Then we are really *not* free, then we are only a tiny particle of dust, continually thrown around in the vast mill of the universe, trying in vain to persuade itself that it is free. Freedom is the foundation of everything, and we too can be free *only* if he is the Creator. When our freedom bows before him, it is not taken away: only then is it really accepted and made definitive. But there is something else on this day that we are celebrating: the One we worship is not some remote power. He himself has knelt before *us* to wash our feet. That gives our adoration a relaxed quality, an atmosphere of hope and joy, because we are bowing before him who has bowed before us; because in bowing we are entering into a love which does not enslave but transforms. Let us ask the Lord to give us this awareness and this joy so that, from this day on, it may radiate far into our land and into our daily lives. Amen.

MAY DEVOTIONS
Memories and Reflections

A Spirituality Involving
Color and Sound

For me, as no doubt for most Catholics, "May Devotions" awaken many memories. I see the decorated church, filled with the scent of spring flowers; there are the candles and the hymns with their message of warmth, sincere affection and trust. Here the sober laws of liturgical form do not apply; instead we have the simple piety of ordinary people, who love color and sound and strong feeling. The mood of springtime informs the church's interior; nature's blossoming, the warm air of May evenings, human gladness in a world that is renewing itself—all these things enter in. Veneration of Mary has its place in this very particular atmosphere, for she, the Virgin, shows us faith under its youthful aspect, as God's new beginning in a world that has grown old. In her we see the Christian life set forth as a youthfulness of the heart, as beauty and a waiting readiness for what is to come.

Of course all this can be dismissed as sentimentality. But is it not the case that our age suffers from a violent suppression of the emotions? Not only is it unable to mourn; it also has an inability to experience joy. This suppression of feeling leads to a coldness of mind and a brutalization of the heart. Some people object that the kind of things I have mentioned show Christianity penetrated by paganism. This is actually nature-religion, they say, the cult of spring, symbolized in the figure of the young woman to whom the name "Mary" has been given. It is only a very superficial and external "christening" of something that, in reality, is essentially no different from the cult of Artemis or Diana: the eternal cult of the freshness and beauty of the virgin. Call her what you like, it is ultimately the cult of Mother Earth and her fertility.

In my view we need to look at things from exactly the opposite angle. In Mary the earth has acquired a human face, and more: a Christian face, the face of the Mother of Jesus. By turning to her, nature-spirituality is transformed into faith, into an encounter with God's dealings with men in history, which bear their destined fruit in Mary's life, in the Incarnation of God. So it is quite in order to say that, in Mary, faith and nature-religion have been reconciled. It seems to me that a pusillanimous fear of paganism inhibits and threatens our faith, just as does the fear of sentimentality, which has long since turned into a rationalistic "complex".

Of course there *is* a paganism that is opposed to Christ and which, in the form of fear of mysterious powers or as the worship of creatures, enslaves human beings. But there is also a nature-spirituality that expresses man's genuine nature and is a response to the nature of creation. To suppress *this* kind of nature-religion would be to trample on the human heart as it waits and looks for Christ; it would be to cut off the human roots of faith.

We ought here to reappropriate the perspective of Cardinal Newman, which was also the perspective of the Fathers. In the similarities between Christian and pagan worship, Christian and pagan thought, Newman sees, not a proof of Christianity's dependence on paganism, but an indication that, throughout his entire history, man has been waiting for Christ. Man was being prepared for Christ.

On one occasion he says this: "And, accordingly, that the Gospel is in certain points like the religions which preceded it, is but an argument that 'God is one, and that there is none other but He' " (*Parochial and Plain Sermons* 5:170).

In a particular way, the figure of Mary illustrates the unity of the Old and New Testaments, but she also links nature-religion and faith. That is not a weakness of Marian devotion: it is an important basis of it; it corresponds to the historical significance of the Mother of the Lord. As the Fathers put it, she is the Christian earth, the earth that bore Christ. Through her, nature-spirituality has acquired a face, and a history which opens out into Christ, and so it has been baptized. The truth in it has come to the surface, and now, full of joy, it can bloom in God's garden of faith. Nature-spirituality may unfold without any anxiety in the Marian sphere because its orientation to the Mother of the Lord has rendered it entirely Christian. In the same way paganism, in spite of the aberrations that distort and deface it, has not simply fallen into the void: we can say that Artemis and Diana, Devaki and Kvannon, or whatever the respective pagan figures may be called, have now found their right name and have been purified by it. The mists of expectation have given way before historical reality.

Furthermore, the misplaced fear of paganism which inhibits Christian faith not only suppresses the emotions and severs the connection between faith and nature; it also robs woman of her place in the Christian edifice. The kind of emancipation which is being put forward today in technologically based cultures is crying out for women at last to become men. But this is not equality of rights: it is the ultimate oppression of women by a civilization in which the hegemony of technology implies the subjugation of nature and the subjection of women—the two are closely interrelated. Both features originate in part, no doubt, in a form of Christianity which, in its flight from paganism, has led to a new and more dangerous, post-Christian paganism.

The proper response to such stunted development is devotion to Mary, whom faith rightly calls "Mother of God". For the reasons we have given, this devotion is of great importance for a healthy faith. Of course we do not think about all this in May devotions; it is simply there, with faith's inner instinct. And it is precisely because the dowry of nature-religion has not been lost but has become Christian that these devotions have a lighthearted atmosphere of warmth and trust.

2

Marian Contemplation Leads to the Heart of the Mystery

So far we have been reflecting on the form of Marian spirituality found in May devotions. We took for granted its biblical basis, which was expressed in more indirect terms. Now, in turning explicitly to this biblical source, we shall acquire new perspectives and deepen what we have already considered. And indeed, contrary to the widespread view, the biblical witness to Mary is so rich that it cannot be exhausted in a few sentences. I shall only select a single aspect, closely connected with what we have already said.

Next to John, as is well known, it is above all Luke who is the interpreter of the Marian mystery. He stresses one particular feature of the picture of Mary which was important to him, and thus became important for the tradition which has come down through him, when he says three times that Mary kept the word in her heart and pondered it (Lk 1:29; 2:19; 2:51). First of all, then, she is portrayed as a source of the tradition. The word is kept in her memory; therefore she is a reliable witness for what took place. But memory requires more than a merely external registering of events. We can only receive and hold fast to the uttered word if we are involved inwardly. If something does not touch me, it will not penetrate; it will dissolve in the flux of memories and lose its particular face. Above all it is a fact that understanding and preserving what is understood go together. If I have not really understood a thing, I will not be able to communicate it properly. Only by understanding do I receive reality at all; and understanding, in turn, depends on a certain measure of inner identification with what is to be understood. It depends on love. I cannot really understand something for which I have no love whatsoever. So the transmission of the message needs more than the kind of memory that stores telephone numbers: what is required is a memory of the heart, in which I invest something of myself. Involvement and faithfulness are not opposites: they are interdependent.

In Luke, Mary stands as the embodiment of the Church's memory. She is alert, taking events in and inwardly pondering them. Thus

Luke says that she "kept" them (lit., "preserved them together") in her heart, she
"pondered" them (lit., "put them together")
and "kept them faithfully" (lit., "held on to
them"). Mary compares the words and events
of faith with the ongoing experience of her
life and thus discovers the full human depth
of each detail, which gradually fits into the
total picture. In this way faith becomes understanding and so can be handed on to others:
it is no longer a merely external word but
is saturated with the experience of a life,
translated into human terms; now it can be
translated, in turn, into the lives of others.
Thus Mary becomes a model for the Church's
mission, i.e., that of being a dwelling place
for the Word, preserving it and keeping it
safe in times of confusion, protecting it, as it
were, from the elements. Hence she is also
the interpretation of the parable of the seed
sowed in good soil and yielding fruit a hun-
dredfold. She is not the thin surface earth
which cannot accommodate roots; she is not
the barren earth which the sparrows have
pecked bare; nor is she overgrown by the
weeds of affluence that inhibit new growth.
She is a human being with depth. She lets the
word sink deep into her. So the process of
fruitful transformation can take place in a
twofold direction: she saturates the Word

with her life, as it were, putting the sap and energy of her life at the Word's disposal; but as a result, conversely, her life is permeated, enriched and deepened by the energies of the Word, which gives everything its meaning. First of all it is she who digests the Word, so to speak, transmuting it; but in doing so she herself, with her life, is in turn transmuted into the Word. Her life becomes word and meaning. That is how the gospel is handed on in the Church; indeed, it is how all spiritual and intellectual growth and maturity are handed on from one person to another and within humanity as a whole. It is the only way in which men and mankind can acquire depth and maturity. In other words, it is the only way to progress.

This brings us back to our earlier questions. Today, by progress we generally mean the growth in the scope of technology and the increase in the gross national product. When we say progress, quite simply, we think of "having" more.

The psychoanalyst Erich Fromm, who died recently, adopted Gabriel Marcel's distinction between "being" and "having" and refashioned it into a clear opposition: either "being" *or* "having". He saw the sickness of our civilization in our compulsion to change everything into "having"; but if we are to "have" something, it must be already dead, for we can only "have" things that are inert. Consequently he described our civilization, which is a civilization of "having", as a civilization of necrophilia—in love with death and dead things. Perhaps that was extreme. But we can say that mere progress at the level of "having" turns, quite consistently, into a progress [*Fortschritt*, lit., "a step forward"] toward death. In such a case, the speed of progress must necessarily show a terrifying aspect. Progress in "having", unless it is matched by progress in "being", is deadly. But we can only achieve progress at the level of "being" if, inwardly, we are deepened through contemplation, in which we open ourselves to meaning, assimilate it and so ourselves become assimilated to meaning, become meaning-full. In the long run a civilization without contemplation cannot survive.

Far less can the Church survive without contemplation! In our activity-oriented, one-sidedly masculine, Western Christianity, contemplation is more and more undervalued. The loss of contemplation, moreover, is largely identical with the loss of the Marian aspect. We have been trying to justify Christianity primarily on the basis of deeds. But where "being" is trampled underfoot, our deeds soon become monstrous.

And as they were eating, he took bread
and blessed and broke it
and gave it to them and said,
"Take, this is my body."

Mark 14:22

Last Supper. Book of Gospels from Great St. Martin's,
Cologne (c. 1230), Ms 466/9222, fol. 7v. Brussels,
Bibliothèque royale Albert 1er.

Our *theology*, too, exhibits a frightening lack of contemplative depth. In general it is far removed from the words of Ignatius of Antioch: "Anyone who truly possesses the words of Jesus will also be able to hear his silence . . . that he may act through his word and be known through his silence" (Eph 15:2). When theology no longer hears the silence of Jesus, it can even less discern the depth of his words. With its all-too-technical methods it is sorely tempted to treat the Word like some inert chattel; the living Lord is scarcely audible.

Thus the increasing loss of the Marian element in the Church only serves to underline once again how necessary it is. The Church must be a realm of quiet, a place of meditation and silence. She lives by the heart's memory, which penetrates to the core of things and so opens them to understanding. This is the only way in which man can enjoy real progress, progress not only in "having" but in depth of "being". And it is precisely through Marian contemplation, which is not always trying to produce things and yield measurable results, that the Church ministers to man. For by doing so she causes the Word of God to penetrate the world, that meaning without which all our possessions are nothing but dead weight.

MEDITATIONS AT VACATION TIME

I

Going in Search

One of the remarkable facets of our modern civilization is the reappearance of the nomadic element: every weekend entire columns of automobiles stream out of the towns, only to return to their points of departure on Sunday evening, along roads that are hopelessly jammed. When it is vacation time, this phenomenon becomes a veritable mass migration; an entire nation seems to be on the road. In the so-called highly developed countries, the roads are among people's most frequented locations, and the money currently invested in them is an indication of the state of mind that causes people to become restless wanderers. What is the reason for it?

Clearly, people do not feel really at home in their houses and apartments. Many of them get out of their "home" as quickly and as often as they can. The house seems to be more an expression of the prison of everyday life than a place of security where one is glad to be. We can suggest, therefore, that this escape to four wheels indicates a yearning to throw off the constraints of the workaday world and to embrace freedom, the open spaces, an entirely different milieu, a place where, at last, one can be oneself in creativity and freedom. This regular mass migration on the part of industrial society thus expresses something very profound about man and human nature. He cannot be completely at home among his possessions. He is driven by an unrest, yearning for something more, something bigger. He is looking for a freedom that transcends the freedoms and fulfillments of settled life.

Cannot we see here something of the truth of what the Bible says about man being a pilgrim in this world, unable completely to find a home in it? Surely we can discern here something of that restlessness of heart of which Augustine speaks—Augustine, who had been a restless seeker, unsettled and driven about, until he finally grasped why nothing was enough for him. Today's nomad may feel that the automobile (and *auto* is the Greek word for "self") is an expression of his freedom and self-determination, something that is irreplaceable quite apart from its functional usefulness. But does it give him selfhood and freedom, or does it not in fact force him back into the rat race?

So our vacation habits could lead us to take a good look at ourselves and encourage us to embark on a more momentous adventure than we generally envisage. Surely the journey which is really worthy of man is that which takes him out of everyday constrictions in the search for the Eternal, the search for the face of God, and hence enables him to transcend all earthly limitations. And might this not result in man discovering both freedom and a sense of being at home?

2

The Search for Real Life

During the excavations of the lost Roman civilization in North Africa in the last century, an inscription of the second or third century was discovered in the marketplace of Timgad in Algeria. It says: "Hunting, bathing, playing, laughter—this is life." I always think of this inscription every year when the columns of holidaymakers stream south—in the search for life. When, in years to come, people excavate the billboards advertising our vacation pursuits, they will find a similar picture of life set forth on them. Evidently most people experience their year in the office, in the factory or elsewhere as simply not living. On vacation we set off, to be free at last, to live at last. Swimming, playing, laughing—that is life. This is the promise which persuades people to join the long lines of southbound automobiles; if there is life to be found, it is worth exercising the necessary patience.

This aspiration to relaxation, freedom and a stepping out of the everyday routine is absolutely human. Given the pace of modern technologically oriented life, these pauses for breath are simply a necessity. This granted, however, we also have to admit that we have problems with our freedom, with the freedom that leisure time gives us. Most suicides take place, as has been shown, on Saturdays and Sundays—in leisure time. Released from the automated atmosphere of the world of work, man suddenly feels unable to cope with living. He discovers that swimming, playing and laughing are not, after all, life. The more leisure we have for living, the more it becomes evident that we do not know what living is. The question of coping with leisure, with vacation time, is beginning to become a new field of study.

Apropos of this I recall that Thomas Aquinas wrote a special treatise on the means of combating sadness. He takes as his starting point a sentence from the wisdom books of the Old Testament: He who increases knowledge, increases sorrow (Qo 1:18). We can see this rather clearly in our technological world, which has sought to release people from sorrow by means of scientific progress. What does Thomas recommend? It is evidence of his realism that he, too, mentions bathing, sleeping and amusements. The reason he gives is that bathing and sleeping are conducive to the proper state of bodily movement and that every good disposition of the body has an effect on the heart as the center of all movement, both mental and physical.

To that extent Thomas agrees with the Timgad inscription and with what we find on our vacation posters. But he would not describe this as "life", nor would he say that, in bathing, playing, laughing and sleeping, we have reached the goal of our search for lost life. His analysis goes further in that he also mentions being together with friends as a means of combating sadness, for it disperses the loneliness which breeds discontent. Above all, leisure ought to mean that we have time for our fellow men.

Ultimately however, for Thomas, an indispensable remedy against sadness is that we should occupy ourselves with truth, i.e., with God. This is contemplation, in which man is in touch with real life. If we exclude contemplation from our vacation program, even this free time will be still unfree; assuredly we shall not succeed in our search for lost life. The search for God is the most exciting excursion into the mountains, the most invigorating "swim" a man can have. Swimming, playing, sleeping—all this is part of vacation, and I wish you plenty of sunshine and peace as well. But with Thomas Aquinas I would ask you to include the meeting with God in your holiday plans. Our beautiful churches and God's beautiful world invite you to this meeting. And above all I wish you much joy in it and that it will bear fruit in a refreshment that will last beyond the vacation period and affect everyday life throughout the whole year.

3

Take Time to Rest

For the Seventeenth Sunday in Ordinary Time (Year B), the new lectionary of the Catholic

liturgy has selected a Gospel that shows us
how even the disciples of Jesus had to face
the problem of stress and recuperation (Mk
6:30–34). The apostles return from their first
mission, full of what they have experienced
and achieved. They are totally preoccupied
with recounting their successes; in fact, it has
become a whole business operation, and things
have gone so far that, with all the coming and
going, they no longer have time to eat. Perhaps
they are expecting to be congratulated on
their zeal; but instead, Jesus summons them
to go with him to a solitary place where they
can be alone and rest.

I believe it is good that we should discern
the humanity of Jesus in an event like this; he
is not always uttering sublime words only,
nor is he constantly wearing himself out in
order to deal with everything that forces
itself upon him. I can just imagine his face as
he says these words; whereas the apostles are
positively beside themselves and, full of zeal
and self-importance, neglect their meals,
Jesus brings them down from the clouds:
Have a rest for awhile! One can sense his
quiet humor, his friendly irony as he brings
them down to earth. It is precisely in this
humanity of Jesus that his divinity becomes
visible; here we see visibly what God is like.
Any kind of hectic activity, even in religious

affairs, is utterly alien to the New Testament picture of man. We always overestimate ourselves when we imagine we are completely indispensable and that the world or the Church depends on our frantic activity. Often it will be an act of real humility and creaturely honesty to stop what we are doing, to acknowledge our limits, to take time to draw breath and rest—as the creature, man, is designed to do. I am not suggesting that sloth is a good thing, but I do want to suggest that we revise our catalogue of virtues, as it has developed in the Western world, where activity alone is regarded as valid and where the attitudes of beholding, wonder, recollection and quiet are of no account, or at least are felt to need some justification. This causes the atrophying of certain essential human faculties.

All this is illustrated by our use of leisure time. Often it is nothing but a change of scene, and many people would be ill at ease if, afterward, they did not plunge once more into the mass and return to their work routine— from which they originally wanted to escape. That is why it is so necessary for us, who live constantly in an artificial world of man-made things, to leave it behind and seek to encounter creation in its natural state.

I would like to mention a small but significant thing of which the Holy Father spoke in his retreat addresses for Paul VI. There he tells of his conversations with a scientist, "a first-class research scientist and a fine man", who told him: "Scientifically, I am an atheist . . ."; yet the same man once wrote to him: "Whenever I am confronted with the majesty of nature, of the mountains, I feel that *he* exists."[7]

God does not come to light in the artificial world of man-made things. So it is all the more necessary for us to leave our workaday world behind and go in search of the breath of creation, in order that we may meet *him* and thus find ourselves.

[7] K. Wojtyla, *Zeichen des Widerspruchs* (Freiburg, 1979), 22.

MISCELLANEOUS

I

Play and Life

Every four years the world soccer champion-
ship proves to be an event that captures the
imagination of hundreds of millions of people.
Practically no other event on earth has such a
widespread effect. It indicates that some fundamental human aspect is being addressed.
What is it?

The pessimist will say that it is the same as
in ancient Rome: bread and circuses for the
masses. Bread and circuses—this is what the
life of a decadent society amounts to, unaware
as it is of any higher functions. But even if we
accept this observation, it is not sufficient as
an explanation.

Let us ask again: what is the fascination
of the game, that it can acquire the same
importance as bread? Looking at ancient
Rome again, we could say that the call for
bread and circuses is really an expression of
the yearning for a paradisal life, a life of
satisfaction without toil, a life of fulfilled

freedom. For ultimately that is what a game is: it is something entirely free, without utility or necessity, yet which exercises and fulfills all man's capacities.

Thus we could see the game as an attempt to return to paradise by stepping out of the enslaving seriousness of everyday life and the need for self-preservation and into the free seriousness of something that *does not have to be*, and for that very reason has a certain beauty. In some respects, therefore, the game goes beyond everyday life. Yet initially, on the other hand (and particularly in the case of children), it has a different aspect: it is a training *for* life. It symbolizes life itself, anticipates it, as it were, in a freely created form.

It seems to me that the fascination of soccer lies in the fact that it combines these two aspects in a very convincing form. First of all it obliges man to discipline himself, so that, through training, he masters himself; through self-mastery he achieves excellence, and through excellence, freedom. Above all, soccer teaches him to work together with others in a disciplined manner; the team game compels the participants to insert their individual contribution into the whole. The team is united by the common aim; the individual's success and failure lies in the success or failure of the whole team. Finally it teaches fair play toward the opposition; the mutually accepted rules actually bind together and unite the opposing sides; and, once the game is over (provided it has been properly played), the free seriousness of "opposition" during the game gives way to the freedom of a game that is over. The spectators identify themselves with the game and the players and so participate in the teamwork and the battle of skills, in both the seriousness and the freedom of the game. The players become symbols of one's own life, and this has a reciprocal effect on them: they know that people feel represented and affirmed by them.

Of course all this can be spoilt by a mercenary spirit that subjects the whole game to the baneful seriousness of money and turns it from a game into an industry, creating an imaginary world of frightening proportions. But even this imaginary world could not exist apart from the positive rationale that underlies the game, namely, to be an anticipation of life and a transcendence of life in the direction of a paradise lost. In both cases the fundamental thing is the search for a discipline of freedom; through adherence to the rules we learn how to work together with and against others and how to cope with ourselves. It could be that, as we reflect on these things, the game could actually give us a new approach to life itself. For it brings to light fundamental considerations: man does not live by bread alone; indeed, the world of bread is ultimately only the preliminary stage leading to what is really human, the world of freedom. But freedom lives by rule and discipline, which teach us how to live together and how we should legitimately oppose one another; they teach us to be independent of external success and personal whim and thus to be genuinely free. The game is *life*—if we examine it more carefully, the phenomenon of a world devoted to soccer could give us more than mere amusement.

2

Open and Closed Churches

Some years ago a poster could be seen outside many churches of the Alpine foothills, and its message is still worth considering: it showed the mighty porch of the old minster of Frauenchiemsee with the two lion heads on the door, on guard, as it were, at the entrance to the sanctuary. In the picture the door is half-open: the lions are watchful, but they do not forbid entrance to anyone who is in harmony with the spirit of the house of

God. Thus the church in the picture is both open *and* protected; the lion that both guards it and grants admission is that generally accepted reverence for holy things which is more valuable than bolts and bars since its protection operates from within.

Down the centuries our churches have been able to stay open, protected in this way; no one needed to worry about the precious things that were always there for all to see. Today attempts are being made, through street festivals, to make culture public, available once more to people who cannot or will not buy tickets for the theatre or concerts. Until now the most beautiful form of culture, public and available to all, was to be found in our open churches. One of the pioneers of modern art at the end of the nineteenth century wanted his pictures to hang, not in the museum, but in the railway station; he had forgotten that the Western world did not need that kind of proletarian revolution, because it had long possessed a community "House of Beauty" (and at a much higher level) in the church, where art is not the privilege of the few nor an expression of the past but a living presence, a shared center of life that sustains everyone and radiates into their daily lives. Today, however, we are in danger of losing all this; it is a sign of spiritual collapse, ultimately signaling the decline from civilization into barbarism. The traveller increasingly finds himself confronted with locked doors today: the symbolic lion is no longer adequate; in its place, now, is the bolt. In recent years the robbery of works of art from our churches has become more systematic; not infrequently the thieves are people who know what they are looking for, stealing selected pieces with the help of antique collectors' catalogues. What once was a common inheritance thus becomes a private ornament; what was sacred becomes the paraphernalia of self-aggrandizement; what was a living presence becomes the object of a dabbling with past culture.

We cannot be happy with a situation where the churches are locked in order to safeguard a common heritage. It means that we have given in to this negative trend. It means that the Church has ceased being what she once was and that we have lost that shared, sacred center of life where we are all open to each other, where God and the world of the saints are open to us. It means that the Church has capitulated to the laws of this aeon, to the principle that all things can be bought, that everything is subject to market forces, we ourselves included. On the above-mentioned poster, therefore, putting the symbol into words, we read: Help to keep our churches open as places of quiet and prayer.

In the turmoil of the Second World War,

Reinhold Schneider wrote these words: "It is only those who pray who can stay the sword that hangs over our heads." This applies here in a very practical sense: only the presence of people at prayer can protect the Church from within; it alone can keep her open. For the fate of the church building symbolizes the fate of the living Church. The locked church building stands for a Church that can no longer be open from within because she can no longer confront the negative spirit of the age. To that extent it is by no means the concern of Christians only; it is a question of whether we, all of us, can succeed in living together in a genuinely human way. The truth of Cardinal Faulhaber's dictum that the culture of the soul is the soul of culture is demonstrated here in a tangible way. Locked and plundered churches should be an alarm signal to us, sending us back to cultivate the soul before it is too late.

3

Peace

In recent times the word "peace" has in many ways become the watchword at the center of the political and moral issues animating our society. The picture, however, is an appalling one: not infrequently the struggle for peace is carried on with violence against persons and things. It is noticeable that the call for external peace is accompanied by the lack of inner peace.

In the face of these events, a prayer from the Roman liturgy strikes me with increasing force and relevance: "Deliver us, Lord, from every evil, and grant us peace in our day." These words follow the last petition of the Our Father: Deliver us from evil. Jesus intended the whole weight of the Our Father to rest on the initial petition: Thy kingdom come. But very soon men found this request too lofty and remote. Their experience led them to change the emphasis. So now *their* petition was the last one, and it no longer meant "Deliver us from the evil one" but was more all-inclusive: "Deliver us from evil" —from all evil, from the burden of the past, the pressure of the present, the ill fortune of the future. The conclusion of the Our Father became the cry of all human distress for help, for a change for the better. We can see how this particular emphasis so dominated the attitude of Christians in the way the Roman and several other liturgies took up this petition and developed it into an entirely new prayer. It was probably Gregory the Great who gave it its final form in the Roman

Missal; he also added the reference to peace and thus interpreted deliverance from evil as a request for peace. In the background we can discern the tumultuous times in which he had to rule: Rome had become a powerless provincial city, ceaselessly racked by the horrors of the wars brought about by migrating peoples; it experienced the loss of peace as the epitome of all evils.

Our age more and more resembles that of Gregory, and so this prayer has once more become particularly relevant. Thus the final petition of the Our Father is in a very special sense *our* prayer. But in praying it, we ought to bear in mind that, in Jesus' view, it was only a variation of the first and second petitions: the world is delivered from the evils of the absence of peace to the extent that it becomes God's kingdom, i.e., insofar as God reigns in it and his standards are acknowledged. Only then can we tackle the lack of peace. But God's standards can only be applied if God lives within men and women, if his reality is the determining power in their lives. And there is something else: the evil from which we ask to be delivered is, in the mind of Jesus, primarily and most importantly the loss of faith. For Jesus, the inability to believe in God and to live by faith is the evil of all evils. All others result from it—the scorning of human dignity, the destruction of trust between people, violence, the rule of egoism and the loss of peace. Peace can never last on earth if God becomes meaningless to people. Christian efforts for peace must therefore concentrate, among other things, on making clear the hierarchy of values and the hierarchy of evils. Working for peace must mean teaching people to recognize what makes for peace. Consequently it must be an education for the kingdom of God, teaching people to hallow his Name, for otherwise God's image, the human being, will not be held holy. For the sake of the goal it has in view, Christian peace work must particularly seek to counter the evil seen in the destruction of faith and the loss of an awareness of God. For only the kingdom of God can effectively counter war and violence; only where God's kingdom comes near can peace grow and flourish. Prayer, therefore, is an essential part of Christian efforts for peace. "Deliver us from evil. Deliver us from every evil and give us peace in our day."

4

Concern for God's Creation

Francis of Assisi has a preeminent place in the calendar of saints of the Catholic Church. This man is loved by Christians and non-Christians, believers and unbelievers alike. He radiates a cheerfulness and a peace that situate him beyond many otherwise irreconcilable antagonisms. It is natural, of course, that succeeding generations have read into him their own particular dream of the "good man". In an age that began to tire of the dispute between the confessions, he seemed to represent a supra-confessional Christianity that had thrown off the wearisome burden of history and begun again, quite simply, with the Jesus of the Bible. Later he was adopted by the Romantic movement, where he was reinterpreted as a kind of nature enthusiast. Today Francis is seen differently again, and this is connected with two factors that influence the consciousness of people throughout the industrialized nations. In the first place there is fear; fear of the unforeseeable consequences of technological progress. And in the second place we have a bad conscience on account of our high standard of living in the face of hunger in the world. What is fascinating about Francis, therefore, is his resolute renunciation of the world of possessions and his unaffected love for creation, for the birds, the fish, fire, water, earth. He appears as the patron saint of conservationists, the leader of the protest against an ideology based solely on production and growth rates, as the advocate of the simple life.

There is truth in all these pictures of Francis; everywhere he touches the nerve of some problem of human existence. But if we look more closely at Francis he will provide a corrective to our ideas at all points. He does not simply confirm them; he is much more demanding than we would like to think, and he challenges us to face the demands of truth itself. Thus, for instance, we cannot solve the problems of Christian division simply by running away from history and creating our own Jesus.

It is the same with other issues. Take the question of the environment, for instance. There is a story that goes as follows: Francis told the brother responsible for the garden never to plant the whole area with vegetables but to leave part of the garden for flowers, so that at every season of the year it may produce our sisters, the flowers, out of love for her who is called "the flower of the field and the lily of the valley" (Song 2:1). In the same way he wanted there always to be a particularly beautiful flower bed, so that, at all times, people would be moved by the sight of flowers to praise God, "for every creature calls to us: God has made me for thy sake, O man" (*Mirror of Perfection* 11:118). We cannot take this story and simply leave the religious element to one side as a relic of a bygone age, while accepting its refusal of mean utility and its appreciation of the wealth of species. This would in no way correspond to what Francis did and intended. Above all, however, this story contains none of the bitterness that is directed against human beings (for their alleged interference in nature), such as one detects in so many conservationist manifestos today. When man himself is out of joint and can no longer affirm himself, nature cannot flourish. On the contrary: man must first be in harmony with himself; only then can he enter into harmony with creation and it with him. And this is only possible if he is in harmony with the Creator who designed both nature and us. Respect for man and respect for nature go together, but ultimately both can only flourish and find their true measure if, in man and nature, we respect the Creator and his creation. The two only harmonize in relationship with the Creator. We shall assuredly never find the lost equilibrium if we refuse to press forward and discover this relationship. Let Francis of Assisi, then, make us reflect; let him set us on the right path.